Cast Iron Cooking

QUARRY

Saffron-Lamb Tagine with Rosemary, page 56

Pan-Seared Filet Mignon with Fusilli and Cilantro-Pecan Pesto, page 46

Mussels in Lager Broth, page 111

Rustic Berry Skillet Galette with Almonds, page 74

Skillet Steak alla Pizziaola, page 43

Apple-Raisin Skillet Bread Pudding, page 23

50 Gourmet-Quality Dishes
from Entrees to Desserts

Cast Iron Cooking

Dwayne Ridgaway

QUARRY BOOKS

First published in the United States of America by
Quarry Books, a member of
Quayside Publishing Group
100 Cummings Center
Suite 406-L
Beverly, Massachusetts 01915-6101
Telephone: (978) 282-9590
Fax: (978) 283-2742
www.quarrybooks.com

Library of Congress Cataloging-in-Publication Data
Ridgaway, Dwayne.
   Cast iron cooking : 50 gourmet-quality dishes from entrees to desserts /
Dwayne Ridgaway.
      p. cm.
   ISBN 1-59253-237-3 (pbk.)
   1. Cookery, American. 2. Cookware. 3. Cast-iron. I. Title.
TX715.R572 2006
641.5'89—dc21

2005030181
CIP

ISBN-13: 978-1-59253-237-7
ISBN-10: 1-59253-237-3

10 9 8 7 6 5 4 3 2

Design: Wilson Harvey, London
Layout and Production: Q2A Solutions
Cover Image and Photography: Allan Penn Photography

Printed in Singapore

Burgundy Beef Stew, page 106

Contents

Stir-Fried Steak and Peppers with Chimichurri, page 60   Grilled Cornflake-Crusted French Toast, page 78

Pineapple-Coconut Skillet Upside-Down Cake, page 35

Skillet Macadamia-Crusted Mahi Mahi with Papaya-Ginger Relish, page 31

Blackened Scallops with Sauvignon Blanc–Lemon Caper Sauce, page 20

Skillet Pork Tenderloin with Balsamic-Cider Jus and Caramelized Leek and Fennel Salad, page 24

Introduction

Tracing Cast Iron through History

Cast iron has a rich culinary history that has weathered the test of time. The earliest known cast iron dates from seventh- and eighth-century Europe. Sixteenth-century European emigrants brought heirloom-quality tools with them as they traveled to discover and settle new lands. Though much else was left behind, seldom did a traveller arrive without the family's cast-iron cookware. Cast-iron cookware was so valuable that it is said that some families specified the recipient in their wills.

Cast iron was quite literally responsible for feeding thousands of people. With fire as the only means of cooking, cast iron was invaluable to the preparation of every meal— a valuable commodity because of its durability, large cooking capacities, and heating qualities. Anything could be prepared in cast iron, from cakes and pies to stews, roasts, chilis, and succotash. So popular were these pots and pans that wagons were constructed with specific compartments for particular shapes of cast-iron cookware.

In 1896, Joseph Lodge began what is now probably the most popular name on true black cast-iron cookware, Lodge

Manufacturing, and in doing so launched what remains a culinary revolution. Few developers, designers, and manufacturers can truly say that something they made one hundred years ago is still in use today. And quite literally the cast iron that was turned out in Lodge's small production plant along the Tennessee River one hundred years ago is still with families and turning out home-cooked meals across America.

Less than thirty years later, in a factory in Northern France, Le Creuset began producing its own line of cast iron cookware. Each piece is made from molten steel and cast in a unique mold, then enameled in bright colors by

French craftsmen. The resulting cookware, well known among chefs and culinary experts worldwide, can be used for marinating, stove top and oven cooking, or food storage.

Over the years, cast iron had managed to outlive and out-perform a barrage of cookware inventions. The natural quality of cast iron to conduct heat in a way that is uniform, with no hot spots, is what makes it so popular—that, and the natural nonstick nature of cast iron after many uses. If cared for properly and consistently, cast-iron cookware will develop a natural nonstick surface that puts Teflon to shame. Whether used over a campfire, stovetop, or in the oven, the cooking quality of cast iron tops that of most other cookware made of other materials.

Today, cast iron's growing popularity has led to the development of numerous pots and pans for just about every cooking technique. Most recently available on the market are the cast-iron tagines for North African–style cooking, and cast-iron woks, which if you think about it makes perfect sense. The cone-lidded tagine retains steam to turn out long-cooked stovetop stews and casseroles that are juicy and succulent. A wok's traditional purpose is to heat up evenly for fast, hot cooking. A cast-iron wok does this perfectly and develops a natural nonstick coating that improves after every use, making stir-frying a breeze.

From bakeware and roasting pans to skillets of every size and shape, cast iron is enjoying a culinary renaissance, claiming a new spot in every household kitchen. I have developed this book to take a step away from the Old World toward creating more modern classic recipes for cast iron cooking, and giving today's cook a new realization of the many uses of and ways to enjoy cast iron. With proper care and maintenance, the cast iron of today will last for generations to come, as will these recipes.

Keeping classic techniques and easy preparation in mind, I offer recipes that explore new flavors and interesting combinations, using a variety of cast-iron pans. With many recipes focusing on the cast-iron skillet in varied dimensions, from Pan-Fried Striped Bass with Orange-Mustard Sauce and Kickin' Shrimp Scampi with Linguine to Five-Spice Pork Tenderloin and Blackened Beef Tenderloin with Gorgonzola-Chive Mashed Potatoes, they may make our forefathers turn in their graves, but I think they would soon wish that they had these ingredients available. Encompassing the classic cast-iron skillet as well as the wok, tagine, griddle, and grill pan, these recipes and ingredients explore flavors traditional and modern, including ingredient combinations and cooking techniques that may not be so common. I don't think you would have found Ginger-Lime Scallops with Bok Choy and Roasted Red Pepper Salad on

Pan-Fried Striped Bass with Orange-Mustard Sauce, page 50

Cast-Iron Texas Chili, page 118

the table hundreds of years ago, but you may have found a version of a Black Pot Osso Buco or a hearty Cast Iron Texas Chili. Either way, I think you will find a recipe or two in here that may remind you of your grandmother's cast-iron cooking or that give you reas on to find your own cast iron way of living.

As a professional and home cook, I have used many pieces of cookware over the years, none of which have come close to the quality of cast iron. In some way

or another I have worked on this book for many years, simply because I remember, as a child, watching my grandmother, mother, and sister work together over the stove preparing in my great-grandmother's cast-iron Dutch oven Shrimp Gumbo (the Creole way), and realizing then that I loved cast-iron cookware. That Dutch oven (see photo, page 10) was passed on to me and I use it today in much of my home cooking, as well as many other heirloom pieces of black and enamel-coated cast iron.

chapter 1

Cast Iron Basics

Plum and Almond Skillet Cobbler with Ginger Topping, page 28

Choosing Your Cast Iron

There is no magic behind choosing cast-iron cookware. Just find a reputable maker and choose a model that is suitable for what you cook most often. If I had to suggest a "starter" set of cast-iron cookware, it would consist of the following: a 10¼" (25.6 cm) skillet with a lid, a 10¼" (25.6 cm) -deep skillet (with 3" [7.5 cm] sides) with a cover; a round or square grill pan; a 10½" (26.2 cm) round griddle; and a 5-quart (4,750 ml) Dutch oven with lid. A set like this, depending on the maker, will probably cost you around $150 (in the U.S.)—

which, imagining the lifetime or more it will last, is not much to invest. The versatility a set like this offers is endless. Between frying, roasting, sautéing, and grilling, there are endless cooking techniques available to you, from just these few pieces.

I have numerous pieces of cast iron in my arsenal of cooking equipment and the most used by far is my 10¼" (25.6 cm) black skillet. Making stovetop and oven cooking equally easy, this skillet has developed a natural nonstick coating. With proper care and use, you too will have a great

set of cast iron that will never need replacement. Popular today not only in classic black but also with vibrantly colored enameled coatings, cast iron is not only practical but has become quite attractive, serving almost as showpieces in many kitchens. More costly than black, enamel-coated cast-iron cookware will give you the same characteristic cooking traits as classic black pans with the difference being in the look and care of the product. Most popular in enamel-coated cast iron is Le Creuset, a French maker of truly heirloom, colorful

pieces of quality that, with proper care and use, are worthy of being passed along to the next generation. Whatever your style preference, choose your cast iron wisely and treat it as an investment, understanding that the cost is minimal when a lifetime of enjoyment is in front of you.

Proper Care and Use of Your Cast Iron

Contemporary cast-iron cookware has stayed true to its original qualities of hardened iron with tremendous cooking advantages; some pieces have stood the test of time for centuries and are still in use today. The changes made to cast-iron cookware over the years are few but important for the ease of today's cooking. While most true, black cast iron cookware still needs to be seasoned and properly cared for, there are new lines of cookware that are "preseasoned," going straight from the box to the stove. Lodge, the most trusted cast iron producer, in my opinion, has introduced Lodge Lodgic and ProLogic Factory Seasoned Cast Iron that can be used for cooking as soon as it's unpacked. I suggest buying this any time it is available, simply because of the immediate usability and the even "seasoned" coating it comes with.

Seasoning Original-Finish Cast Iron

"Seasoning" is the process by which the gray, porous iron absorbs vegetable oil into its surface, turning the iron black and slick. Repeated over time, this not only produces a smooth, nonstick surface but lends flavor to every meal. To season classic cast iron, follow these simple steps:

1. Preheat the oven to 350°F (180°C, or gas mark 4).
2. Wash new, natural-finish cast iron with hot, soapy water, using a stiff brush or scrubbing sponge. Rinse and dry thoroughly. Always use a cotton dish towel to dry cast iron—paper and terrycloth towels will leave residue and list on the rough surface of the nonseasoned pan.
3. Coat all of the interior and exterior surfaces with melted solid vegetable shortening or vegetable oil.
4. Place the cookware on the middle rack of the oven, lining the lower rack with aluminum foil to catch any drippings. Bake for 1 hour, then turn the oven off, leaving the cookware in the oven until cool.

Once it has cooled, the cast-iron cookware will look slightly brown but will be seasoned and ready to use. To turn the cookware darker, you may repeat the process two or three more times. Be sure to run your vent hood, as the seasoning process causes quite an odor. The more you use your cast iron the more seasoned it becomes, eventually developing a rich, smooth, black surface.

Caring for Factory-Seasoned Cast Iron

Rinse the new cast iron with hot water (do not use soap) and dry thoroughly. Before using to cook, prepare the cooking surface by oiling or spraying with vegetable oil spray. After every use, wash the cast iron thoroughly under hot water (do not use soap) and dry completely (I suggest drying all cast iron in a hot oven after washing). Rub the inside evenly with a thin coat of vegetable oil or spray, and store.

General Care for Your Cast-Iron Cookware

Properly cared-for cast iron will last more than a lifetime. For many decades of enjoyment, just follow these simple tips:

Cleaning After every use, wash the cast-iron cookware under hot water, using a stiff brush. Never wash seasoned cast iron with soap or detergent, as these will deteriorate the seasoned surface. Avoid putting hot cast iron into cold water, as it may cause the pan to crack or warp. After every washing, towel-dry the cast iron thoroughly and place in a hot stove or on a stovetop burner to dry completely.

After drying, coat the inside surfaces of the cast-iron dish evenly with a thin layer of vegetable oil or spray, rubbing it into the surface.

Storage Store your cast iron in a cool, dry place. If you have a lid for the pan, place a folded paper towel between the lid and the base to allow air to circulate.

Rusting If you notice signs of rust on your cast iron, simply scrub with hot water and soap, removing the rust, and reseason the dish.

One joy of cast iron is the vintage nature of its appeal. Finding old pieces of cast iron in an estate sale or antique store is often possible. Creating your own "heirloom" collection of vintage cast-iron pieces could be fun. However, many times, older, used pieces of cast iron have some damage or rust. Pick only those pieces that appear to you to be easily manageable, meaning with minimal rust and little or no damage. Such damage as cracking or warping is not an easy fix, though signs of rusting is—just follow the tips above on getting rid of the rust and reseasoning the surface. Names you may recognize on vintage cast iron are Lodge, Griswold, and Wagner. These are three names that can trace their heritage back generations, to when cast iron was forging its way through culinary history. Be assured that quality is behind every product made by these manufacturers and that finding a good, gently used piece will provide a lifetime of cooking pleasure.

chapter 2

Cast-Iron Skillet **Cooking**

Kickin' Skillet Scampi with Linguine, page 44

The Versatile Skillet

The skillet has become the most-used cast-iron piece in my house and probably the most popular in many kitchens. Professional chefs consider cast-iron cookware to be a precision tool that allows for accurate control of food temperatures. The natural characteristic of conducting heat evenly makes a cast-iron skillet perfect for any stovetop. I recently purchased a flat-top range. For this surface, it is important that skillets have a flat, even surface. Every cast iron piece that I have has a flat, even bottom and works great on the flat-top range. Be cautious, however, of the weight of cast iron pieces when using on a glass-top range. Damage to the range top can be costly.

Cast-iron skillets come in many sizes and shapes from 6" to 17" (15–42.5 cm), round, oval, square, and everything in between. Additionally, the enamel-coated styles come in many colors. In this chapter, I have included something for every type of skillet. If you are buying only one, I suggest the versatile and readily available 10¼" (25.6 cm) round cast-iron skillet. Manufactured by a variety of makers, this size skillet is one that will give you years of enjoyment. I know of one that has been in my family for generations.

Skillet **Scallion Biscuits**

When I was a child, biscuits were a regular breakfast treat, usually dripping with butter and honey or preserves, or toasted and topped with cheese. Baking biscuits in a cast-iron skillet develops a crisp bottom that gives them a great bite. Use these scallion biscuits either for breakfast, topped with scrambled eggs and gravy, or as a savory dinner side with baked ham.

2 cups (220 g) all-purpose flour

1 tablespoon (4.6 g) baking powder

1 teaspoon (4 g) sugar

1 teaspoon (6 g) kosher salt

1/4 cup (50 g) vegetable shortening

1 cup (235 ml) buttermilk

1/2 cup (50 g) chopped fresh scallions, white and green parts

1 egg mixed with 1 tablespoon (14 ml) water for egg wash

Preheat oven to 375°F (190°C, or gas mark 5).

Combine the flour with the baking powder, sugar and salt in the bowl of a mixer fitted with the paddle attachment. Add the shortening and mix on medium speed until a mealy consistency is reached. Mixing on low, gradually add the buttermilk, until just combined. Add the scallions and mix just enouth to incorporate. Empty the dough onto a lightly floured work surface and knead into a rectangular shape. Roll the dough, with a floured rolling pin, to about a 1/2" (12.5 mm) thick rectangle. Cut out rounds using a 2 1/2" (6.25 cm) round biscuit cutter. Drop the biscuits in the bottom of a well-seasoned, lightly oiled 10" (25 cm) cast-iron skillet. Brush the tops with the egg wash and bake for 20 to 25 minutes, until the tops are browned and the insides are firm. Serve warm.

[Serves 6]

Blackened **Beef Tenderloin with Gorgonzola-Chive Potatoes**

6 (6-8 ounce [170-225 g]) beef center-cut tenderloin steaks

¹/₂ cup (120 ml) teriyaki sauce

2 tablespoons (28 ml) Worcestershire sauce

1 teaspoon (14 ml) liquid smoke

¹/₄ cup (60 ml) soy sauce

1 tablespoon (6 g) coarse ground black pepper

2 tablespoons (15 g) blackening seasoning

¹/₄ cup (60 ml) vegetable oil

FOR THE POTATOES:

2 pounds (1 kg) Yukon gold potatoes, cut into large chunks

4 tablespoons (55 g) butter

3 tablespoons (45 ml) heavy cream

1 teaspoon (6 g) kosher salt

¹/₂ teaspoon (1 g) black pepper

¹/₃ cup (40 g) crumbled Gorgonzola cheese

¹/₄ cup (25 g) chopped fresh chives

In a large bowl combine the teriyaki sauce with the Worcestershire sauce, liquid smoke, soy sauce, and black pepper. Place the tenderloin steaks fully submerged in the marinade; cover and refrigerate for at least 2 hours or overnight.

Place the potatoes in a large pot filled with water. Bring to a boil, then cook potatoes until tender when pierced with a fork, about 20 minutes. Drain the potatoes, leaving them behind in the pot, and add the butter, heavy cream, salt, and pepper. Using a potato masher, mash to a thick puree. Add Gorgonzola cheese and chives, stirring to combine and melt the cheese, cover, and set aside, keeping warm.

Remove the steaks from the marinade and pat dry. Coat evenly and generously with blackened seasoning. Heat vegetable oil in a large cast-iron skillet over medium-high heat. Add the steaks in one even layer, searing for 7 minutes per side (for medium rare), 10 minutes per side for medium and 12 minutes per side for well done. If you like your steaks medium or well done, reduce the heat to medium so as not to burn them. Transfer to serving plates with the mashed potatoes.

Blackened **Scallops with Sauvignon Blanc–Lemon Caper Sauce**

There is no better cooking skillet for the technique of blackening than well-seasoned cast iron. Blackened catfish is a tremendously popular Southern cast iron dish that is good any day of the week. But not to bore you with the same old dish, I used scallops here with a pan sauce that just gobbles up all the seasonings left behind. However, if you prefer catfish (or any other firm white fish) certainly use it instead.

DRY RUB:

1 teaspoon (2.5 g) blackening seasoning

1/2 teaspoon (1.5 g) garlic powder

1/4 teaspoon (0.5 g) cayenne pepper

1/4 teaspoon (1.5 g) salt

1/4 teaspoon (0.5 g) freshly ground black pepper

1/2 teaspoon (3 g) Lawry's seasoning salt

2 pounds (1 kg) large sea scallops

3 tablespoons (40 g) butter, plus 4 tablespoons (55 g) cut into cubes and kept cold

1/2 cup (120 ml) sauvignon blanc wine

Juice of one lemon

4 cloves garlic, minced

2 tablespoons (17 g) capers

In a small bowl combine the dry rub ingredients. Place the scallops in a large bowl and toss with the dry rub mixture, coating evenly and thoroughly. Melt 3 tablespoons (40 g) of butter in a 10" (25 cm), well-seasoned cast-iron skillet over medium-high heat. Once melted, add the scallops, cooking for 5 minutes on each side until browned. Remove scallops and set aside.

Deglaze the pan with the white wine and lemon juice, stirring to capture all the bits from the bottom of the pan. Add the garlic and capers, stirring and cooking for 2 minutes. Gradually add the remaining cold butter, two or three pieces at a time, stirring vigorously to emulsify the sauce after each addition of butter. Serve the scallops topped with the pan sauce.

Apple-Raisin Skillet Bread Pudding

One of my favorite desserts is bread pudding, a simple preparation that produces a delicious comfort food. Baking in a cast iron skillet or pan (as shown) creates a lovely crust around the edges of the bread pudding.

$^1/_2$ cup (82 g) golden raisins

$^1/_4$ cup (60 ml) dark rum

$^1/_3$ cup (75 g) unsalted butter, cut into cubes

4 cups (200 g) day-old Portuguese sweet bread, torn into pieces

$^1/_2$ cup (100 g) sugar

3 eggs, beaten

1 $^1/_2$ cups (355 ml) milk

1 $^1/_2$ teaspoons (7.5 ml) vanilla extract

$^1/_2$ teaspoon (2.5 ml) lemon extract

$^1/_2$ teaspoon (1.25 g) ground cinnamon

1 tart apple, cored and cubed

FOR APPLE BUTTER DRIZZLE:

$^1/_2$ cup (112 g) unsalted butter

$^1/_2$ cup (120 ml) apple butter

$^1/_4$ cup (60 ml) dark spiced rum

In a small bowl combine the raisins and rum, and let steep for 30 minutes. Meanwhile, preheat the oven to 325°F (170°C, or gas mark 3). Place butter in the bottom of an 8" (20 cm) square cast-iron baking dish or a 9" (22.5 cm) round cast-iron skillet and place the dish in the hot oven, melting the butter. Once the butter is melted, remove the dish and place the torn bread pieces inside, tossing them around to coat evenly with the melted butter, then set aside. In a mixing bowl whisk together the eggs and sugar with the milk, vanilla and lemon extracts, and cinnamon. Add the soaked raisins with their liquid and the cubed apple. Pour over the bread, tossing gently to distribute the fruit evenly throughout the bread. Let stand for 5 minutes while the bread absorbs some of the moisture. Bake on the center rack of the oven until a knife inserted in the middle comes out clean, about 50 to 60 minutes. Remove and set aside. In a small saucepan over medium heat melt the butter, add the apple butter and spiced rum, and cook until the alcohol is cooked off and the mixture is thickened, about 5 minutes. Serve warm drizzled over individual servings of the bread pudding.

Skillet **Pork Tenderloin with Balsamic-Cider Jus and Caramelized Leek and Fennel Salad**

A favorite in my house is Asian-inspired pork tenderloin. Traditionally, I grill this dish but have adapted it here for a cast-iron skillet. The result is tender, juicy, and, quite frankly, darn good.

2 teaspoons (5 g) five-spice powder

1/2 teaspoon (3 g) salt

1/2 teaspoon (1 g) coarsely ground black pepper

1 teaspoon (2.5 g) ground dried mustard

1 teaspoon (5 g) sugar

2 (1–1 1/2 pound [455–670 g]) pork tenderloins, trimmed of fat and silverskin

3 tablespoons (40 g) butter, divided

1 tablespoon (14 ml) vegetable oil

1/4 cup (60 ml) balsamic vinegar

1 cup (235 ml) apple cider

3 leaves fresh sage

3 juniper berries

2 tablespoons (28 ml) olive oil

2 leeks, white and tender green parts only, thinly sliced

1 fennel bulb, thinly sliced

1 tablespoon (13 g) sugar

Salt and pepper, to taste

1/4 cup (15 g) chopped fresh flat-leaf parsley

2 tablespoons (3.5 g) chopped fresh tarragon

2 tablespoons (5 g) chopped fresh chives

In a small bowl combine the five-spice powder, salt, black pepper, dry mustard, and sugar. Rub the pork tenderloins evenly and thoroughly with the five-spice mixture. Cover and set aside for at least 30 minutes, or refrigerate overnight.

Preheat oven to 400°F (200°C, or gas mark 6). Melt 1 tablespoon (14 g) of the butter with the vegetable oil in a 10" (25 cm) well-seasoned cast-iron skillet over medium-high heat. Add the tenderloins, browning on all sides for a total of about 12 minutes. Add balsamic vinegar, apple cider, sage leaves, and juniper berries. Place in the oven and bake for 20 minutes, or until a meat thermometer reads 135°F (57°C). Remove, transfer tenderloin to a cutting board and pan sauce to a gravy boat. Wipe out the skillet.

Heat 2 tablespoons (28 ml) of olive oil with the remaining 2 tablespoons (28 g) of butter over medium-high heat. Add the leeks and fennel and cook for 4 minutes. Reduce heat to medium, sprinkle with sugar and season with salt and black pepper, then cook for an additional 20 minutes until browned and caramelized. Remove from heat and toss with parsley, tarragon, and chives. Slice tenderloin into medallions, serve atop fennel salad drizzled with pan jus.

[Serves 4]

Skillet **Ponzu Salmon with Wilted Greens**

Ponzu is an Asian citrus-scented soy sauce perfect as a marinade, dressing, or sauce for dipping. I use it along with mirin (sweetened sake) to develop a perfect balance of sweet, salty, tart, and tangy for pan-seared salmon and wilted greens.

1/4 cup (60 ml) ponzu sauce

1/2 cup (120 ml) mirin

1/4 cup (60 ml) pineapple juice

1 tablespoon (8 g) grated fresh ginger

1 teaspoon (2 g) coarsely ground black pepper

1 tablespoon (14 ml) lemongrass oil (or other vegetable oil)

2 pounds (1 kg) salmon fillet, cut into 4 steaks

1 teaspoon (2 g) toasted sesame seeds

1 teaspoon (2 g) black sesame seeds

4 tablespoons (60 ml) extra-virgin olive oil, divided

4 cups (80 g) mixed greens, such as mustard greens, watercress, Swiss chard, and baby spinach

3 cloves garlic, minced

1/4 cup (55 g) toasted pine nuts

Salt and pepper, to taste

1 cup (110 g) julienned parsnips

1 cup (130 g) julienned carrots

4 tablespoons (55 g) Cilantro-Chile Butter (recipe follows)

2 cups (330 g) cooked jasmine rice

FOR CILANTRO-CHILI BUTTER:

1/2 cup (112 g) unsalted butter, softened

1/2 teaspoon (1.5 g) ancho or chipotle chile powder

1/2 teaspoon (2.5 ml) lime juice

In a small bowl combine the ponzu with the mirin, pineapple juice, ginger, pepper, and lemongrass oil; whisk lightly to combine. Place the salmon in a shallow dish and pour the marinade over it. Cover and refrigerate for at least 1 hour. Remove the salmon from the refrigerator 30 minutes prior to cooking and sprinkle with sesame seeds. Heat 2 tablespoons (28 ml) of olive oil in a large, well-seasoned cast-iron skillet over medium-high heat. Place the salmon fillets in the skillet and cook for 10 minutes per side until browned and the flesh begins to flake; reduce the heat if necessary so as not to burn the fish. Remove, transfer to a plate, and keep warm.

To the hot skillet add 2 tablespoons (28 ml) of olive oil; when hot, add the greens with the garlic and pine nuts, tossing them about the pan to wilt for 3 minutes, and season with salt and pepper. Remove and transfer to a platter. Heat the remaining 1 tablespoon (14 ml) of olive oil in the pan, add the parsnips and carrots, season with salt and pepper, and sauté until tender, about 6 minutes.

To serve, form the jasmine rice into four rounded mounds using a ramekin or glass coated with nonstick cooking spray and place in the center of a plate. Top the jasmine rice with the wilted greens, placing the salmon alongside topped with Cilantro-Chile Butter and julienned vegetables.

[For Cilantro-Chili Butter]
In a small bowl, using a fork, combine the butter with the chile powder and lime juice. Transfer the butter mixture to a piece of plastic wrap and roll into a cylinder shape, and freeze or refrigerate for 30 minutes, until firm. Slice off pieces as needed to use as a topping for grilled or pan-fried fish, poultry, and beef.

Plum and Almond Skillet Cobbler with Ginger Topping

A cobbler can be a combination of almost any stone fruit or berry you like. If you can't find plums or nectarines, substitute peaches, pears, or a mix of berries equaling the same amount as used in the recipe, replacing the almond extract with pure vanilla extract for a variation in flavor as well.

Butter, for greasing pan

FOR FILLING:

4 cups (900 g) pitted and quartered plums

2 cups (400 g) pitted and sliced nectarines

1/2 cup (75 g) firmly packed light brown sugar

1 tablespoon (8 g) all-purpose flour

1 teaspoon (2.5 g) finely grated lemon zest

1/2 teaspoon (1.25 g) ground cinnamon

1/2 teaspoon (2.5 ml) almond extract

Pinch of salt

FOR TOPPING:

1 1/4 cups (140 g) all-purpose flour

1/3 cup (65 g) sugar

2 teaspoons (3 g) baking powder

1/2 teaspoon (1.25 g) ground cinnamon

1/4 teaspoon (1.5 g) salt

2 tablespoons (20 g) finely chopped crystallized ginger

1 egg

1/2 cup (120 ml) buttermilk

6 tablespoons (83 g) unsalted butter, melted and cooled

1/2 teaspoon (2.5 ml) vanilla extract

1/2 cup (60 g) sliced almonds

Preheat oven to 375°F (190°C, or gas mark 5). Lightly grease with butter a 2-quart (1 L) enamel-coated cast-iron skillet or baking dish. Prepare the filling; in a mixing bowl, gently toss the plums and nectarines with the sugar, flour, lemon zest, cinnamon, almond extract, and salt. Pour the mixture into the prepared skillet or baking dish.

[For topping]

In a bowl stir together the flour, sugar, baking powder, cinnamon, salt, and ginger. In a separate bowl whisk together the egg, buttermilk, butter, and vanilla extract. Pour the wet ingredients into the dry. Using a rubber spatula, fold the mixtures together until a soft dough is formed. Drop heaping

spoonfuls of the topping randomly over the fruit, leaving spaces to expose the fruit. Finish by sprinkling the top with sliced almonds. Bake until the filling is bubbling and the topping is browned and firm, about 45 minutes. Serve warm with ice cream and whipped cream.

[Serves 6]

Skillet **Macadamia-Crusted Mahi Mahi with Papaya-Ginger Relish**

Mahi mahi is a firm white fish great for grilling, baking, and pan-frying. Cast-iron skillets are perfect for pan-frying or searing fish, as the excellent heat and the seasoned characteristic of the skillet develop a caramelized crust on the fish's outer flesh. This recipe is finished in the oven so as not to burn the topping but cook the fish to a tender flakiness.

6 (6-ounce [170 g]) fillets mahi mahi

2 teaspoons (6 g) grated fresh ginger

Juice of 2 limes (about $^{1}/_{3}$ cup [80 ml])

1 tablespoon (1.7 g) chopped fresh tarragon

3 cloves garlic, minced

1 cup (235 ml) papaya nectar

$^{1}/_{2}$ cup (120 ml) olive oil

$^{1}/_{2}$ teaspoon (1.5 g) ancho chile powder

$^{1}/_{4}$ teaspoon (0.75 g) onion powder

$^{1}/_{8}$ teaspoon (0.25 g) allspice

$^{1}/_{8}$ teaspoon (0.25 g) ground coriander

$^{1}/_{2}$ teaspoon (1 g) ground black pepper

$^{1}/_{2}$ teaspoon (3 g) salt

1 tablespoon (20 g) honey

2 tablespoons (20 g) brown sugar

1 cup (135 g) finely chopped macadamia nuts

3 tablespoons (42 ml) vegetable oil

FOR THE PAPAYA-GINGER RELISH:

1 papaya, seeded, peeled, and chopped (about 1 cup [175 g])

1 mango, seeded, peeled, and chopped (about 1 cup [175 g])

3 scallions, chopped

1 teaspoon (3 g) grated fresh ginger

$^{1}/_{3}$ cup (40 g) chopped fresh red bell pepper

Juice of one lime

$^{1}/_{4}$ cup (60 ml) papaya nectar

Salt and black pepper, to taste

In a large bowl combine the grated ginger, lime juice, tarragon, garlic, papaya nectar, olive oil, ancho chile powder, onion powder, allspice, coriander, black pepper, salt, honey, and brown sugar; stir to combine. Add the mahi mahi fillets, cover, and refrigerate for one hour. Meanwhile, prepare the relish by combining the papaya, mango, scallion, ginger, red pepper, lime juice, and papaya nectar. Season with salt and black pepper, toss to combine, cover, and refrigerate until the fish is ready for serving.

To prepare the fish, remove from the refrigerator 15 minutes prior to cooking. Preheat oven to 375°F (190°C, or gas mark 5).

Heat the vegetable oil in a large cast-iron skillet on the stovetop over medium-high heat and add the fish fillets in a single layer, browning for 5 minutes. Turn the fish, topping the browned side with the macadamia nuts in an even, packed coating. Remove from heat and place in the preheated oven; bake until the macadamia nuts are browned and the fish is flaky, about 20 minutes. Remove and serve topped with the cold Papaya-Ginger Relish.

[Makes 12 slices]

Apple-Cranberry Cornmeal Skillet Cake

Like pineapple upside-down cake, this dessert is baked in a well-seasoned cast-iron skillet and inverted onto a serving platter, presenting a delicious, caramelized, and gooey topping that is great with vanilla ice cream.

3/4 cup (175 ml) whole milk

1 cup (138 g) coarsely ground cornmeal

1/2 cup (112 g) unsalted butter

1 cup (150 g) dark brown sugar

2 Granny Smith apples, peeled, cored, and sliced into 1/4" (6 mm) -thick wedges, tossed with 1 tablespoon (14 ml) lime juice

1/2 cup (55 g) fresh or frozen cranberries

1/3 cup (33 g) chopped pecans, toasted

3 tablespoons (42 ml) orange juice

1 cup (110 g) all-purpose flour

2 teaspoons (3 g) baking powder

1/2 teaspoon (3 g) salt

3 eggs

3/4 cup (150 g) sugar

1 teaspoon (14 ml) vanilla extract

1/8 teaspoon (.25 g) ground nutmeg

1/2 cup (120 ml) canola oil

Preheat oven to 350°F (180°C, or gas mark 4). In a small saucepan heat the milk over medium-high heat just until steaming and bubbling. Stir the cornmeal into the milk, set aside, and let rest for 30 minutes. Melt the butter in a 10" (25 cm) seasoned cast-iron skillet over medium heat. Once melted, add the brown sugar, stirring until dissolved, about 5 minutes. Remove the skillet from heat and carefully place the apple slices in barely overlapping concentric circles in the center of the skillet, working outward. Dot the apples with cranberries and sprinkle with pecans. Drizzle orange juice over the top.

In a large mixing bowl whisk together the flour, baking powder, and salt. In a separate bowl whisk the eggs until light. Add the sugar, vanilla, and nutmeg to the eggs and whisk to combine. Add the canola oil to the egg mixture and whisk. Add the cornmeal mixture to the egg mixture, whisking to combine. Add this mixture to the flour mixture and stir to combine. Pour the batter over the apples and cranberries, smoothing to an even layer with a rubber spatula, and bake for 45 minutes. Remove and let rest for 30 minutes. Invert the cake onto a platter or cake plate and serve with whipped cream or vanilla ice cream.

[Serves 8]

Pineapple-Coconut Skillet Upside-Down Cake

Upside-down cake is a classic cast-iron dish that, while baking, caramelizes in the skillet to create a gooey, tasty topping that, when inverted, oozes down the sides, moistening every bite. This dish combines the traditional pineapple with coconut, rum, and the unique flavor of cardamom. Inspired by island cooking, these flavors are tropical in approach and mouthwatering in taste.

FOR TOPPING:

6 tablespoons (83 g) unsalted butter

3/4 cup (170 g) packed light brown sugar

1 (15-ounce [440 ml]) can sliced pineapple

FOR BATTER:

1/2 cup (112 g) unsalted butter, softened

1 cup (200 g) granulated sugar

3 large eggs

1 teaspoon (5 ml) vanilla extract

1 tablespoon (15 ml) coconut-flavored rum

1 1/2 cups (165 g) all-purpose flour

1 1/2 teaspoons (3.5 g) ground cardamom

2 teaspoons (3 g) baking powder

1/4 teaspoon (1.5 g) salt

1/2 cup (120 ml) unsweetened pineapple juice

1/4 cup (17 g) coconut flakes, plus 1/4 cup (17 g) toasted for garnish

Preheat oven to 350°F (180°C, or gas mark 4).

[For topping]

Melt the butter in a well-seasoned 9" (22.5 cm) cast-iron skillet over medium-high heat. Add the brown sugar and melt, stirring constantly, until bubbling, about 6 minutes. Remove from heat, add pineapple rings in one even layer, and set aside.

[For batter]

Beat the butter in a large bowl with an electric mixer until light and fluffy. Add the sugar and beat until creamy. Add the eggs, one at a time, beating well after each addition. Beat in vanilla and coconut rum. In a separate bowl, combine the flour, cardamom, baking powder, and salt. Add half of the flour mixture to the egg mixture and beat on low speed just until blended. Add the pineapple juice and beat on low to incorporate, add remaining flour mixture, beating until just incorporated. Spoon the batter over the pineapple, smoothing the top evenly. Bake on the center rack of the oven until golden brown and a skewer inserted in the middle comes out clean, 45 minutes to 1 hour. Remove from the oven and let stand for 5 minutes. To remove from the skillet, run a sharp knife around the edge to release the sides. Invert a cake plate or service platter over the skillet and invert the cake onto plate, keeping pan and plate firmly pressed together. The cake should drop from the skillet onto the plate. Drizzle the cake with additional coconut rum, top with toasted coconut flakes, and serve.

[Serves 6]

Skillet-**Roasted Venison Backstrap with Blackberry-Thyme Sauce**

The backstrap of venison is the tenderloin, similar to that of pork tenderloin; in fact, if you can't find venison for this dish, certainly substitute pork tenderloin.

2 pounds (1 kg) venison tenderloin, trimmed

1/2 cup (120 ml) port wine

3 (2" [5 cm]) strips orange peel

1/2 teaspoon (1 g) coarsely ground black pepper

1/2 teaspoon (3 g) salt

1/4 teaspoon (0.5 g) ground allspice

4 juniper berries

1 (3" [7.5 cm] long) cinnamon stick

1 bay leaf

1 sprig fresh thyme

2 tablespoons (28 ml) olive oil

1/4 cup (55 g) butter, divided

1/2 cup (60 g) diced leeks

3 shallots, minced

2/3 cup (160 ml) dry white wine

3 tablespoons (60 g) seedless blackberry fruit spread

1 cup (110 g) fresh blackberries

2 sprigs fresh thyme

Place the venison loin in a zip-top sealable plastic bag or sealable container. In a small bowl combine the port wine with the orange peel, salt, black pepper, allspice, juniper berries, cinnamon stick, bay leaf, and thyme. Add the marinade to the bag, moving the venison around to coat evenly. Refrigerate overnight, turning occasionally.

Preheat oven to 400°F (200°C, or gas mark 6). Heat the olive oil in a 9" (22.5 cm) or 10" (25 cm) cast-iron skillet over medium heat, then add the venison, browning on all sides. Transfer the venison in its skillet to the oven and roast for 20 to 30 minutes. A meat thermometer is the best way to judge doneness; for venison tenderloin it should register 160°F (71°C). Remove from oven and allow to rest for 10 minutes.

In a small saucepan over medium-high heat, melt 2 tablespoons (28 g) of the butter. Add the leeks and shallots and sauté until tender and wilted, about 5 minutes. Add the wine, cooking for an additional 12 minutes, or until the liquid is reduced by half. Reduce heat to low and add the blackberry fruit spread and the remaining 2 tablespoons (28 g) of butter, stirring vigorously. Cook until thickened, about 3 minutes. Cut the venison tenderloin into 1/4" (6 mm) -thick slices. Drizzle with blackberry sauce and top with fresh blackberries and thyme.

Ingredients

1/2 pound (225 g) chorizo sausage, crumbled

4 tablespoons (55 g) unsalted butter

1/2 cup (65 g) finely chopped onion

2 tablespoons (32 g) finely diced celery

3 serrano chiles, seeded and minced

1 clove garlic, minced

2 cups (110 g) crumbled cornbread

2 teaspoons (1.5 g) finely chopped thyme

1/2 teaspoon (1.25 g) crumbled dried sage

1/4 cup (5 g) finely chopped cilantro

2 tablespoons (28 ml) half-and-half

1 large egg, lightly beaten

1/4 teaspoon (0.5 g) freshly ground black pepper

2 tablespoons (28 ml) vegetable oil

Two (2 1/2-pound [1 kg]) pheasants

1 bunch fresh thyme

1 bunch fresh sage

1 bunch fresh rosemary

16 cloves garlic, peeled

6 slices smoked bacon

Herb- and Bacon-Roasted Pheasant with Chorizo-Cornbread Skillet Cakes

Mark Miller, famed chef-owner of the original Sante Fe restaurant Coyote Café, inspired this recipe. Miller's ability to combine a robust, southwestern influence with just about any meat or poultry has made him a powerhouse in southwestern cooking circles.

[For cakes]
In a heavy, medium-sized cast-iron skillet cook the chorizo over medium-high heat until browned, about 5 minutes. Transfer to a large bowl. Discard the fat. Melt 2 tablespoons (28 g) of the butter in the skillet, add the onion, celery, serranos, and garlic, and cook until slightly softened, about 3 minutes. Toss the vegetables with the chorizo. Mix in the cornbread, thyme, sage, and cilantro. Stir in the half-and-half and egg. Season with the pepper and mix thoroughly.

Preheat the oven to 400°F (200°C, or gas mark 6). In a large cast-iron skillet (large enough to accommodate both birds) melt the remaining 2 tablespoons (28 g) of butter with the vegetable oil over medium-high heat. Add the pheasants and sear, turning until golden all over, about 6 minutes. Transfer to a plate to cool slightly. Stuff the birds with the herbs and garlic cloves divided between the two. Return the birds to the large cast-iron skillet breast side up; crisscross the top of each bird with three slices of bacon.

Roast until the juices run clear, about 45 minutes. Cover loosely with foil and let rest for 20 minutes before serving.

Meanwhile, shape the cornbread cakes into twelve 2" (5 cm) round patties. Preheat a cast-iron skillet over medium heat with 1 tablespoon (914 ml) of vegetable oil. Add the patties and cook, turning, until lightly browned, 4 to 6 minutes. Carve the pheasants and serve with the patties and any pan drippings.

[Serves 6]

Lime- and Pepper-Seared Shrimp with Black Bean Tamales

Tamales are a staple around Texas where I grew up. They are quite easy to prepare, adding simple creativity to a dish. Use fresh jumbo shrimp for this dish, bouncing them in the hot skillet until just tender and juicy.

FOR THE MARINADE:

1 jalapeño pepper, seeded and minced

1 serrano chile, seeded and minced

1 tablespoon (14 ml) lime juice

2 tablespoons (28 ml) white balsamic vinegar

1 1/2 teaspoons (3.5 g) ground cumin

1/2 teaspoon (3 g) kosher salt

1 tablespoon (6 g) coarsely ground black pepper

1 1/2 pounds (670 g) jumbo shrimp, peeled and deveined

FOR THE TAMALES:

4 cups (900 ml) chicken stock

1 1/4 cups (205 g) polenta

Salt and black pepper

7 dried cornhusks

2 tablespoons (28 ml) olive oil

1 cup (110 g) chopped chorizo

1/2 cup (65 g) chopped yellow onion

2 cloves garlic, minced

1 teaspoon (3 g) dried ground chipotle chile

1 (14.5-ounce [405-g]) can black beans, drained

1/2 cup (82 g) cooked wild rice

3 tablespoons (42 ml) olive oil

2 tablespoons (28 g) butter

1/2 cup (75 g) fresh cooked yellow corn

3 scallions, chopped

1 red tomato, seeded and chopped

1 yellow tomato, seeded and chopped

Juice of one lime

1 tablespoon (1.25 g) chopped fresh cilantro

Sour cream for garnish

In a large bowl combine the jalapeño and serrano peppers with the lime juice, balsamic vinegar, cumin, salt, and black pepper. Add the shrimp and toss to coat; cover and refrigerate for at least 1 hour.

[For tamales]
In a large saucepot bring the chicken stock to a boil and gradually add the polenta in a steady stream while stirring. Reduce heat and cook, stirring until a thickened consistency is reached, and season with salt and black pepper. Remove from heat and set aside. Reserving one dried husk without soaking, prepare six cornhusks by submerging in a large bowl of hot water for 30 minutes. Remove and rinse away any grit, keeping the husks in warm water until ready to use.

In a large cast-iron skillet melt the 2 tablespoons (28 ml) of olive oil over medium-high heat. Add the chorizo with the onion and garlic and cook for 10 minutes, until the chorizo is browned and the onion is

tender. Stir in the chipotle chile and remove from heat; set aside.

To construct the tamales, remove the cornhusks from water and pat dry, then lay out on a clean, dry, flat work surface. Place a heaping scoop of polenta on each husk, press with fingers into the husk to create a well for more ingredients. Add the chorizo and black beans to the well, topping

with the wild rice. Add a small amount of additional polenta on top to seal in the rice, then wrap each husk up and over the filling, creating a pouch. Twist and tie off the ends, using strands from the reserved dry husk. Place a steamer basket in a large saucepot with about an inch of water in the bottom. Place the tamales in the steamer basket (in batches if necessary) and place

over high heat, steaming for 30 minutes, adding additional water to the pot as needed. Remove from the steamer and set aside, keeping warm until ready to serve.

In a large cast-iron skillet, heat 3 tablespoons (42 ml) of olive oil with the 2 tablespoons (28 g) of butter over medium-high heat until the butter is melted. Drain the shrimp from

the marinade and place in the hot skillet, cooking for 10 minutes, tossing so the shrimp cooks and turns pink on all sides. Add the corn, scallions, and red and yellow tomatoes, cooking for 4 minutes. Add the lime juice and cilantro, toss to combine, and season with salt and pepper. Serve the shrimp hot, with the warm tamales, garnished with sour cream.

Swiss Chard and Roasted Pepper Breakfast Frittata

Quiche, pie, strata, or frittata? A frittata is simply a quiche without a crust, baked in a skillet instead of a pie plate. This may not really be a quiche at all but rather an oven-baked, open-faced omelet. Whatever you choose to call it, it is a simple, all-in-one breakfast dish that packs a lot of flavor into one skillet.

1 tablespoon (14 g) butter	1/2 cup (20 g) chopped fresh basil
1 tablespoon (14 ml) olive oil	8 eggs
3 shallots, finely chopped	1/2 cup (120 ml) heavy cream
1 clove garlic, minced	1/4 cup (25 g) grated Parmigiano-Reggiano cheese
1 red bell pepper, roasted, thinly sliced	1 cup (30 g) grated Gruyère cheese
1 yellow bell pepper, roasted, thinly sliced	1/2 teaspoon (3 g) kosher salt
2 cups (40 g) chopped fresh Swiss chard, tough stems removed	1/2 teaspoon (1 g) coarsely ground black pepper

Preheat oven to 375°F (190°C, or gas mark 5). Melt the butter with the olive oil in a 10" (25 cm) well-seasoned cast-iron skillet over medium heat. Add the shallots and garlic and sauté for 3 minutes, until the shallots are tender, being careful not to burn the garlic. Add the roasted peppers and Swiss chard and cook for 3 minutes, until the chard is wilted. Remove from heat and toss in the basil. In a mixing bowl whisk together the eggs with the heavy cream, and Parmigiano-Reggiano and Gruyère cheeses. Season with salt and black pepper and stir. Pour the egg mixture into the skillet with the pepper mixture; gently fold together, evenly distributing the peppers within the eggs. Place on the middle rack of the preheated oven and bake for 50 minutes, until the frittata is puffy and a knife inserted in the middle comes out clean.

4 (6-ounce [50 g])
sirloin strip steaks

1 tablespoon (7.5 g)
Montreal Steak Seasoning

4 tablespoons (60 ml)
olive oil

1 yellow onion, diced

3 Red Bliss potatoes
(about 1/2 pound [225 g])
diced in 1/2" (12.5 mm) cubes

1 green bell pepper,
cored, seeded, and thinly sliced

1 cup (100 g)
sliced cremini mushrooms

1 (14-ounce [395 g]) can artichoke
hearts, drained and chopped

4 cloves garlic,
peeled, thinly sliced

2 tablespoons (17 g) capers

1 (14.5-ounce [405 ml])
can diced tomatoes with basil

2 teaspoons (3.5 g)
fresh chopped oregano, or
1 teaspoon (1.3 g) dried

3 sprigs fresh lemon
thyme, optional

1/8 teaspoon (.25 g) red
pepper flakes

Salt and black pepper

[Serves 6]

Skillet **Steak alla Pizziaola**

Steak and peppers, a tradition as a sandwich. Steak and potatoes, a tradition as comfort food. Combine the two, toss in some Italian flavors, and you have a tremendous Steak alla Pizziaola. You need a very large cast-iron skillet to hold this dish; a 12" (30 cm) pan is recommended or, if you have two 10" (25 cm) skillets, those will work as well. Serve the meal right from the skillets.

Preheat oven to 375°F (190°C, or gas mark 5). Season the steaks evenly with Montreal Steak Seasoning, set aside. Heat the olive oil over medium-high heat in a large 12" (30 cm) cast-iron skillet. When hot, add the steaks to the pan and brown for 5 minutes per side. Transfer steaks to a plate, add the remaining two tablespoons olive oil to the skillet, and heat. When hot, add the onion, potato, green pepper, mushrooms, chopped artichoke hearts, garlic, and capers; sauté for 7 minutes, until the onion is translucent. Add the diced tomato, oregano, thyme, and red pepper, season with salt and pepper, and stir to combine, cooking an additional 2 minutes. Place the steaks on top of the tomato mixture and transfer to the middle rack of the hot oven. Bake for 20 minutes, remove, and serve hot.

[Serves 6]

Kickin' Skillet Scampi with Linguine

My scampi is so easy. They take simply a little prep time with the shrimp but, from there, combine intense flavors into an easy, one-skillet meal. From stove to table, this takes about 30 minutes.

Kosher salt

1½ pounds (670 g) linguine

5 tablespoons (75 ml) good-quality extra-virgin olive oil

6 tablespoons (83 g) unsalted butter

3 tablespoons (30 g) minced fresh garlic (about 8 or 9 cloves)

2 pounds (1 kg) large shrimp, peeled and deveined

½ teaspoon (1 g) coarsely ground black pepper

¼ teaspoon (0.5 g) hot red pepper flakes

¼ cup (15 g) fresh flat-leaf parsley

¼ cup (60 ml) freshly squeezed lemon juice

¼ cup (25 g) freshly grated Parmesan cheese

Bring to a boil a large pot of water seasoned with 1 tablespoon (18 g) of kosher salt, add the linguine, and cook until al dente, 7 to 10 minutes. Drain, run under cool water, drain again, place the linguine back in the pot, and toss with 1 tablespoon olive oil. Set aside, keeping warm. Melt the butter with the remaining olive oil in a large (10" to 13" [25-32.5 cm]) well-seasoned cast-iron skillet over medium-high heat. Add the garlic and sauté for 3 minutes, being careful not to burn. Add the shrimp, 1 teaspoon (6 g) of kosher salt, and the pepper; sauté until the shrimp begin to turn pink, 5 to 7 minutes. Remove from the heat and toss with red pepper flakes, parsley, lemon juice, and Parmesan cheese. Pour the shrimp mixture over the cooked linguine, tossing to combine, and serve immediately.

Pan-Seared **Filet Mignon with Fusilli and Cilantro-Pecan Pesto**

I don't imagine that filet mignon, pesto, and pasta make it to the plate together that often, but here the mixture of flavors is delicious. Melted buffalo mozzarella and pan-roasted tomatoes make a great accompaniment to the tender filet and the bite of the pesto. Make this pesto in large batches to use as a topping or sauce for your other favorite meats, fish, and poultry.

FOR THE PESTO:

3 cloves garlic

2 cups (40 g) loosely packed fresh cilantro leaves

$1/3$ cup (40 g) chopped pecans, lightly toasted

$1/2$ cup (50 g) grated Parmigiano-Reggiano cheese

$1/2$ cup (120 ml) olive oil

2 tablespoons (10 g) Pecorino Romano cheese

1 pound (455 g) dried fusilli pasta

2 tablespoons (28 g) unsalted butter

4 tablespoons (60 ml) olive oil

4 (5- to 6-ounce [140–170 g]) filet mignon steaks, trimmed and cut in half horizontally

Salt and black pepper

1 large ripe red tomato, cut into 4 slices

1 large ripe yellow tomato, cut into 4 slices (optional)

1 large (ovoline) ball fresh buffalo mozzarella (about 4 ounces [115 g]), cut into 4 slices

[Prepare pesto]

In the bowl of a food processor fitted with the blade attachment combine the garlic, cilantro leaves, pecans, and Parmigiano-Reggiano. Pulse to chop the pecans and cilantro, add the olive oil, and pulse to puree the ingredients. Remove, transfer to a bowl, and stir in the Pecorino Romano cheese. Season with salt and black pepper and set aside.

Cook the pasta in a large stockpot of salted boiling water according to package instructions, until al dente, then drain, return to the pot, add 2 tablespoons of butter and almost all of the pesto (reserve ⅛ cup [33 g] for garnish), stir to combine, and set aside.

Preheat the oven broiler to high. Heat 2 tablespoons (28 ml) of olive oil in a 10" or 12" (25 cm or 30 cm) well-seasoned cast-iron skillet over medium-high heat. Season the sliced tomatoes and tenderloin steaks with salt and black pepper. To the hot skillet add the tomato slices in one even layer, cooking (in batches if necessary) until just tender and browned on both sides (only about 3 minutes per side). Do not overcook, or the tomatoes will become mush. Once the tomatoes are cooked, set aside, keeping warm.

Add 2 tablespoons (28 ml) of olive oil to the skillet; when hot place four steaks at a time into the hot skillet and cook until browned on both sides—4 to 5 minutes. Top each steak with a slice of fresh mozzarella. Transfer to a plate and place steak under broiler to melt and brown the cheese, about 3 minutes. While the cheese melts on the first four steaks, place the remaining four steaks on the hot skillet and cook as above. Transfer the cooked, cheese-topped steaks to a plate and keep warm.

Return the pasta to medium heat, add the watercress, and cook for 4 minutes, stirring, until the watercress is slightly wilted and the pasta is warmed. To serve, place the pasta in the center of the plate and top with: cheese-covered steak, a slice of tomato, another piece of steak, then remaining tomato slice. Drizzle with additional pesto and serve.

[Serves 4]

Cajun Blackened Catfish Sandwiches with Watercress

Cookbooks abound with recipes for catfish prepared in cast iron, and there's nothing better than a tender fillet of Cajun-blackened catfish seared in a cast-iron skillet. Cast-iron has an incredible caramelizing effect on meats and seafood. A hot pan with plenty of oil gives a super-crisp caramelized edge to the fish. Enjoy as a sandwich or simply serve with your favorite side.

FOR SPICY RÉMOULADE:

1/4 cup (63 g) mayonnaise

1 tablespoon (15 g) Dijon mustard

2 tablespoons (30 g) sweet relish

1 tablespoon (15 ml) lemon juice

1/2 teaspoon (1.5 g) ancho chile powder

3 tablespoons (23 g) Cajun seasoning (recipe follows)

2 tablespoons (15 g) blackened seasoning

1 pound (455 g) catfish fillets, skinned

4 tablespoons (60 ml) olive oil

4 Portuguese sweet rolls

1 cup (60 g) watercress, divided

FOR CAJUN SEASONING:

2 tablespoons (14 g) paprika

2 tablespoons (18 g) chile powder

1 tablespoon (9 g) granulated garlic

1 tablespoon (6 g) black pepper

1 tablespoon (9 g) granulated onion

1 tablespoon (18 g) salt

1 tablespoon (7 g) cumin

1 teaspoon (7 g) cayenne pepper

2 teaspoons (5 g) dried thyme

2 teaspoons (5 g) dried oregano

1/2 teaspoon (1 g) crushed red pepper flakes

[For rémoulade]

Combine the five rémoulade ingredients in a small bowl, stir to combine thoroughly, cover, and refrigerate. Combine the Cajun seasoning and blackened seasoning, coat each catfish fillet with the seasonings on all sides, rubbing into the flesh, and set aside. Using 2 tablespoons (28 ml) of olive oil, coat the inside of the rolls. Heat an oiled cast-iron skillet over medium-high heat, place the rolls in the pan, oiled side down, and toast until browned, about 2 minutes. Add the remaining 2 tablespoons (28 ml) of olive oil to the skillet. Once the oil is hot, place the catfish fillets in the pan (skin side down) and cook,

flipping once, until well browned on both sides, 5 to 6 minutes per side. Remove from pan, cut each fillet in half, and set aside.

Begin building the sandwiches by spreading rémoulade on the bottoms of the four toasted rolls, and topping with watercress followed by one of the catfish fillet halves. Top with additional rémoulade, place the top roll on each sandwich, and serve.

[For Cajun seasoning]

Combine all the above ingredients in a small mixing bowl, cover in an airtight container, and store for later use.

[Serves 4]

Pan-Fried **Striped Bass with Orange-Mustard Sauce**

If striped bass is only available a short time in your area, substitute any other firm-fleshed fish that you like for this dish. Cod, monkfish, and snapper will all work just as well as striped bass.

2 pounds (1 kg)
striped bass, skinned and boned

$1/4$ cup (30 g) all-purpose flour

1 teaspoon (6 g) salt

1 teaspoon (2 g)
coarsely ground black pepper

2 eggs, lightly beaten

1 tablespoon (14 g)
unsalted butter

$1/4$ cup (60 ml) olive oil

FOR THE SAUCE:

7 tablespoons (200 g)
unsalted butter

4 cloves garlic, minced

$1/4$ cup (60 g) Dijon mustard

$1/4$ cup (60 ml)
fresh orange juice

3 tablespoons (60 g)
orange marmalade

2 teaspoons (5 g) lemon zest

Preheat oven to 375°F (190°C, or gas mark 5). Cut the fish fillets into four equal 8-ounce (225 g) portions. Combine the flour, salt, and pepper in a dish and place the beaten egg in another. Melt the 1 tablespoon (14 g) of butter in a well-seasoned 10" (25 cm) cast-iron skillet with the olive oil. Dredge the fish fillets in the flour, shaking off any excess, then into the beaten egg. Place the fish fillets in the skillet one at a time and sauté until golden brown on both sides, about 5 minutes per side. Transfer from the skillet to a baking dish and bake in the preheated oven for 8 minutes.

While the fish is baking, prepare the sauce: To the olive oil in the skillet, add the 7 tablespoons (200 g) of butter and melt. Add the garlic, mustard, orange juice, orange marmalade, scallions, and zest, blending with a whisk and heating through. Serve the fish fillets topped with sauce.

Zangy Skillet Chicken with Mushrooms and Cipollini Onion

"Zangy" is the best word I could find to describe the flavors of this dish. With its great combination of spicy, sweet, and flavorful ingredients, this will be a crowd-pleaser. I recommend a 13" (32.5 cm) lidded cast-iron skillet for this dish, but smaller batches can be made in a smaller skillet.

1 whole (3-pound [1.3 kg]) roaster chicken, cut into 8 pieces, or 3 pounds (1.3 kg) assorted bone-in or boneless chicken pieces

1 teaspoon (2.3 g) ground cumin

7 tablespoons (100 ml) olive oil, divided

4 tablespoons (55 g) butter, divided

7 whole large white mushrooms, quartered

7 whole large cremini mushrooms, quartered

1/2 cup (50 g) sliced shiitake mushrooms

8 ounces (225 g) cipollini onions, peeled and cut in half

6 cloves garlic, thinly sliced

1/2 cup (120 ml) Madeira

1/4 cup (60 ml) chicken stock

2 large stems fresh rosemary

3 small stems fresh thyme

1 bunch broccoli rabe, trimmed and chopped

Salt and black pepper, to taste

2 tablespoons (40 g) honey

FOR THE ZANGY DRY RUB:

1 tablespoon (9 g) chile powder (ancho or chipotle if you have it)

1 tablespoon (9 g) garlic powder

1 teaspoon (1.3 g) cayenne pepper

2 teaspoons (4 g) coarsely ground black pepper

1 teaspoon (6 g) kosher salt

Place the chicken on a large plate or platter. Prepare the Zangy Dry Rub: in a small bowl, combine the chile powder, garlic powder, cayenne pepper, black pepper, salt, and cumin, stirring to combine. Toss the chicken with the dry rub, coating and rubbing evenly, getting it under the skin; cover and set aside for at least 30 minutes or refrigerate overnight (if refrigerating the chicken overnight, remove 30 minutes prior to cooking).

Preheat oven to 400°F (200°C, or gas mark 6). Heat 3 tablespoons (42 ml) olive oil in a 13" (32.5 cm) lidded cast-iron skillet over medium-high heat. Place the chicken in the skillet in a single layer, browning each side for 5 minutes per side. Remove the chicken and set aside. Add 2 tablespoons (28 g) of the butter and 2 tablespoons (28 ml) of the olive oil to the skillet, melting the butter. Add the mushrooms, onion, and garlic to the skillet. Sauté until the mushrooms are tender and the garlic has begun to brown. Add the Madeira, deglazing the pan and cooking for 2 minutes; add the chicken broth, stirring to combine. Return the chicken pieces to the skillet, with the rosemary and thyme. Toss around to coat the chicken with the pan juices, cover, and place in the preheated oven for 30 minutes, until the chicken is cooked through. Remove and let rest, covered, for 10 minutes.

In a large skillet heat the remaining 2 tablespoons (28 ml) of olive oil with the remaining 2 tablespoons (28 g) of butter over medium-high heat. Add the broccoli rabe, cooking until wilted and tender but still crisp and bright green, about 5 minutes. Season with salt and pepper and add the honey, stirring to combine. Serve the chicken and mushrooms over hot broccoli rabe.

chapter 3

Cast-Iron Wok and Tagine Cooking

Lemon-Orange Chicken Tagine with Cherries, page 58

Global Influences

New to the family of cast iron cookware are woks and tagines, bringing new cultural influences to cast iron cooking. These wok and tagine recipes will excite your palate.

Asian cooking has already become quite popular in American homes and restaurants, most recognizably achieved in a steel wok. However, North African cooking, primarily in a tagine, is something that many homes are not exposed to, either as a flavor or technique.

Offered in enamel-coated cast iron and classic black, seasoned cast-iron woks and tagines are not as common as other cast-iron pots and pans but create a tremendous impact in any kitchen. The tagine makes roasting food a different and fun event. The design of a tagine is such that the moisture of the cooking food remains confined within the vessel, creating a self-basting cooking technique.

The tagine, pictured at left, with the conical, cobalt lid and bowl-like base, is designed to contain ample amounts of condensation on the inside of the lid while still allowing heat and steam to escape during cooking. While this additional moisture ensures a dish's juiciness, the gathering juices may overflow in the dish—always monitor a tagine

dish's progress. The flat-bottom design of the base allows the tagine to be used on any style of stovetop, including gas, electric, or glass induction.

Cast-iron woks are much like their predecessors—steel woks —only better, in my opinion. When fast, hot cooking is needed, cast iron brings its inherent ability to conduct heat in an unprecedented, even manner to the wok. Sturdy construction plus beautiful design and craftsmanship make enamel-coated or black cast-iron woks an eye-pleaser in your kitchen. They bring tremendous versatility as well: not just for stir-frying, woks can be used for sautéing, braising, frying, steaming, and smoking, going from stovetop to oven with ease.

3 tablespoons (42 ml)
olive oil, divided

2 cloves garlic, minced

1 tablespoon (6 g)
peeled, minced fresh ginger

1/4 teaspoon (1 g)
saffron threads

1/2 teaspoon (1.25 g)
ground cinnamon

2 tablespoons (28 ml)
tomato puree

2 tablespoons (7.5 g)
chopped fresh rosemary

2 teaspoons (10 ml) lemon juice

1 tablespoon (15 ml) water

11/2 pounds (670 g) lamb leg,
cut into thick cubes

1 red onion, thinly sliced

1 cup (120 g) zucchini,
sliced into half-moons about
1/2" (12.5 mm) thick

1 cup (130 g) julienned carrot

4 scallions, green and white
parts, chopped

2 tablespoons (8 g)
chopped fresh flat-leaf parsley

Salt and black pepper, to taste

[Serves 4]

Saffron-Lamb Tagine with Rosemary

As with all the tagine recipes, the simple nature of the cooking vessel provides a moist and succulent dish with ample juices and flavor. This lamb is no exception, with a delicious pairing of rosemary and saffron.

In a large bowl combine 2 tablespoons (28 ml) of the olive oil with the garlic, ginger, saffron, cinnamon, tomato puree, rosemary, lemon juice. and water. Add the cubed lamb, tossing to thoroughly combine. Cover and refrigerate for at least 1 hour and up to overnight. Heat the remaining 1 tablespoon (15 ml) of olive oil in the base of the tagine over medium heat. Add the onion and sauté for 6 minutes, until tender; add the zucchini and carrots, and sauté for 3 minutes. Add the lamb with all the herbs and spices to the tagine base and brown for 7 minutes, turning occasionally. Cover with tagine lid and reduce the heat to low. Cook for 2 hours until the lamb is tender. Stir in the scallion and parsley, and season with salt and black pepper, and cook for an additional 15 minutes. Remove cover and serve hot.

1 (3–4 pound [1.3–1.8 kg])
whole chicken, cut into 8 pieces,
bones removed from only
the breasts

1 teaspoon ground turmeric

$1/4$ teaspoon (0.5 g)
ground allspice

1 teaspoon (2.5 g)
ground coriander

$1/2$ teaspoon (1.25 g) paprika

$1/8$ teaspoon (0.25 g)
ground cardamom

$1/2$ teaspoon (3 g) salt

$1/2$ teaspoon (1 g)
fresh cracked black pepper

2 tablespoons (28 ml) olive oil

1 sweet yellow onion, chopped

3 cloves garlic, minced

1 poblano chile, stem and
seeds removed, chopped

1 navel orange, sliced into rings

3 tablespoons (60 g)
orange marmalade

1 tablespoon (15 ml)
white balsamic vinegar

2 tablespoons (28 ml) lemon juice

$1/4$ cup (60 ml) chicken stock

1 packed cup (110 g)
fresh pitted cherries

Salt and black pepper, to taste

Soft Polenta with Feta
(recipe follows)

[Serves 4]

Lemon-Orange Chicken
Tagine **with Cherries**

With a unique domed lid contoured to fit a wide, shallow bowl-style base, a tagine is designed for long, slow cooking. The top is designed to allow moisture to seep back into the dish while cooking, producing a moist, tender, and juicy meal. Be cautious not to overload the dish, as it could cook over during cooking under the pressure of the heat. Only a little added liquid is needed for cooking.

FOR SOFT POLENTA WITH FETA:

2 quarts (1,790 ml) water

1/2 teaspoon (3 g) kosher salt

2 cups (330 g) polenta

1/2 cup (50 g) grated Parmesan cheese

1/2 teaspoon (1 g) cracked black pepper

1/2 cup (75 g) crumbled feta cheese

Place the chicken on a large platter or in a large bowl. In a small bowl combine the turmeric, allspice, coriander, paprika, cardamom, salt, and pepper; stir to combine. Sprinkle the spice mixture over the chicken pieces, coating evenly and thoroughly, rubbing the spices into the flesh and under the skin. Cover with plastic wrap and set aside for 30 minutes. Meanwhile, heat the olive oil in the base of the tagine over medium heat (never cook in your tagine on high heat). Add the onion, garlic, and poblano chile and sauté for 4 minutes, just until tender. Move the onion mixture to the perimeter of the tagine and add the chicken pieces to the center of the pan in batches, browning on both sides, stacking one on top of the other as additional pieces are added. In a small bowl combine the orange marmalade, balsamic vinegar, lemon juice, and chicken stock, and stir to combine. Place the orange slices in and around the chicken pieces, pouring the marmalade mixture on top. Add the cherries, cover, and cook on very low heat for 1 1/2 hours. Remove lid and serve on top of the Soft Polenta with Feta.

[For Soft Polenta with Feta]
In a large stockpot over high heat bring the water to boil with the salt. Once boiling, gradually add the polenta in a steady, slow stream, stirring to incorporate. Reduce heat and stir continuously until the desired consistency is reached; the polenta should be soft, almost like pudding. Remove from heat, add the Parmesan cheese, seasonwith pepper, and stir to combine. Serve, topping with feta cheese.

FOR THE CHIMICHURRI:

1 packed cup (60 g)
fresh flat-leaf parsley

1 packed cup (60 g)
fresh cilantro

3 tablespoons (42 ml)
white wine vinegar

1 tablespoon (15 ml) lime juice

2 tablespoons (7.5 g)
fresh chopped oregano

2 cloves garlic, peeled

$1/2$ teaspoon (1 g)
dried crushed red pepper

$2/3$ cup (160 ml) olive oil

1 (10-ounce [280 g]) package
Asian glass noodles

Salt and coarsely
ground black pepper

2 (12-ounce [340-g])
rib-eye steaks, thinly sliced
against the grain

2 tablespoons (28 ml) olive oil

2 large bell peppers,
preferably red and green or
yellow, roasted and thinly sliced

3 cloves garlic, thinly sliced

1 tablespoon (15 ml)
Asian fish sauce

1 tablespoon (20 g) honey

3 scallions, cut into 3" (7.5 cm)
lengths, sliced into thin strips

1 tablespoon (15 ml) lime juice

[Serves 4]

Stir-Fried **Steak and Peppers with Chimichurri**

Stir-frying is a cooking method that applies high heat to food cooking at a rapid pace. Good-quality beef with a higher fat content, such as rib-eye steak, is great for stir-fried dishes. Cast-iron woks are a new and excellent addition to the cooking scene.

Prepare the chimichurri by combining the first seven ingredients in the bowl of a food processor fitted with the blade attachment. Add the $2/3$ cup (160 ml) of olive oil and puree until almost smooth. Season the chimichurri with salt and pepper; set aside.

Place the Asian glass noodles in a large bowl, add hot water to the bowl just to cover the noodles, and set the noodles aside to soak in the hot water. Season the steak with salt and coarsely ground black pepper. Heat a large, cast-iron wok over high heat. Pour in the 2 tablespoons (28 ml) of olive oil; once glassy and hot add the steak, stir-frying until browned, about 3 minutes. Pull the steak up and to the sides of the wok, add the peppers, garlic, fish sauce, and honey to the bottom of the wok, and stir-fry, tossing vigorously for 2 minutes. Add the scallions, pull the meat into the mixture, then add the lime juice, tossing to combine. Remove from the heat and toss with chimichurri sauce. Drain the glass noodles, shaking off any excess water. Place a mound of noodles on each individual plate and top with the stir-fried beef.

Moroccan Chicken Tagine

Classic Moroccan flavors marry hearty meats with sweet fruits and vegetables, along with powerful herbs and spices offering tang and heat. This tagine dish keeps with this traditional concept of flavor, combining chicken with flavorful vegetables, sweet raisins, and currants, with a punch of herbs and spices.

1½ pounds (670 g) boneless, skinless chicken breast, cut into thick cubes

1 tablespoon (4 g) chopped fresh mint

1 teaspoon (2.3 g) sweet paprika

2 teaspoons (4.6 g) ground cumin

2 teaspoons (4.6 g) ground coriander

¼ teaspoon (0.5 g) cayenne pepper

2 tablespoons (28 ml) fresh lemon juice

3 tablespoons (42 ml) olive oil

½ teaspoon (3 g) salt

1 teaspoon (1 g) ground black pepper

1 red onion, thinly sliced

1 fennel bulb, trimmed and thinly sliced

2 cloves garlic, thinly sliced

½ cup (82 g) golden raisins

½ cup (82 g) currants

1 cup (235 ml) water

2 cups (300 g) cooked couscous

2 tablespoons (7.5 g) chopped fresh cilantro

½ cup (62 g) toasted, sliced almonds

In a mixing bowl toss the chicken with the mint, paprika, cumin, coriander, cayenne pepper, lemon juice, 2 tablespoons (28 ml) of the olive oil, and salt and black pepper. Cover and refrigerate for at least 1 hour and up to overnight. Remove from the refrigerator at least 30 minutes prior to cooking. Heat the remaining tablespoon (15 ml) of olive oil in the base of the tagine over medium heat. Add the onion and fennel bulb and sauté 8 minutes, until tender and aromatic. Add the garlic, raisins, and currants and cook for 3 minutes. Add the chicken mixture to the tagine base and cook for 7 minutes, browning on all sides. Add ½ cup (120 ml) of the water, reduce heat to low, cover, and simmer the dish for 2 to 2½ hours. The spices will thicken the juices, so check after about 1 hour, adding up to ½ cup (120 ml) of remaining water if needed. Serve hot over couscous tossed with cilantro and toasted almonds.

Wok-Seared Ginger-Lime Scallops with Bok Choy and Roasted-Pepper Salad

"Fusion" cooking is a style of cooking that combines Eastern and Western techniques and ingredients to create a delicious meal. The flavors of this dish are truly a fusion of tastes that bounce in your cast-iron wok. Pairing the warmth of roasted peppers with the tang of lime juice and Asian flavors creates a mouthwatering scallop dish to please every palate.

6 tablespoons (90 ml) fresh lime juice

3 tablespoons (42 ml) Asian fish sauce

3 tablespoons (45 g) hoisin sauce

3 tablespoons (45 g) Asian hot chile sauce

3 tablespoons (18 g) grated fresh ginger

1 teaspoon (2.5 g) grated lime zest

24 (about 2 pounds [1 kg]) fresh large sea scallops

Kosher salt and freshly ground black pepper

Olive oil

1 red bell pepper, seeded and thinly sliced

1 green bell pepper, seeded and thinly sliced

1 yellow or orange bell pepper, seeded and thinly sliced

3 scallions, cut into 2" (5 cm) lengths and thinly sliced lengthwise

1/4 cup (15 g) fresh chopped flat-leaf parsley

1/4 cup (15 g) fresh chopped cilantro

1 (10-ounce [280-g]) package frozen corn kernels, thawed and drained

6 heads baby bok choy, cut in half lengthwise

Combine the lime juice, fish sauce, hoisin sauce, chile sauce, ginger, and lime zest in a dish large enough to hold the scallops. Add the scallops, cover, and refrigerate for at least 2 hours. Remove 30 minutes prior to cooking. Brush each pepper with olive oil. Preheat a grill, stovetop gas burner, or broiler to high heat. Roast the peppers over the flame or under the broiler until charred black on all sides. Transfer to a paper bag and close tight; let stand for 5 minutes to loosen the skins. Remove from the bag and remove the skins from the peppers, seed and slice thin, place in a mixing bowl, and toss with the scallion, parsley, cilantro, and corn kernels. Season with salt and pepper and set aside.

Heat 3 tablespoons (42 ml) olive oil in a large cast-iron wok over medium-high heat until glassy and hot. Add the scallops in an even layer and season with salt and pepper, browning on each side for about 4 minutes per side. Remove; set aside. To the hot wok add the pepper salad and heat through. Remove and set aside. Add 2 tablespoons (28 ml) olive oil to the wok, then add the bok choy, cut side down, and brown until tender and wilted. Serve the scallops alongside the bok choy and pepper salad.

Wok-Sautéed **Jumpin' Calamari with Mango Pepperonata**

This wok-prepared take on the Italian classic, pepperonata, is vibrant with crunch and texture from the assorted peppers and the sweetness of summer-ripened mango. Calamari cooks quickly (about one minute), making this a great meal for those on the run.

3 tablespoons (42 ml) olive oil

1 red bell pepper, seeded and thinly sliced

1 yellow bell pepper, seeded and thinly sliced

1 orange bell pepper, seeded and thinly sliced

1 green bell pepper, seeded and thinly sliced

1 red onion, thinly sliced

1 clove garlic, minced

1 jalapeño pepper, seeded and minced

2 pounds (1 kg) calamari tubes, cleaned and sliced into 1/4" (6 mm) rings, tentacles cut in half

1/4 cup (60 ml) pinot grigio

2 tablespoons (28 ml) balsamic vinegar

1 teaspoon (5 ml) lemon juice

1 teaspoon (2.5 ml) lemon zest

1 pinch fresh thyme

2 tablespoons (7.5 g) chopped fresh basil

2 tablespoons (7.5 g) chopped fresh chives

1 teaspoon (1.3 g) chopped fresh flat-leaf parsley

1 pinch red pepper flakes

1 ripe mango, peeled, seeded, and chopped

4 slices sliced ciabatta bread, brushed with olive oil and toasted or grilled, or 4 cups (660 g) cooked sticky rice

Heat 2 tablespoons (28 ml) of olive oil in a cast-iron wok over high heat. When smoking, add the peppers and onion, and sauté stirring briskly for 3 minutes. Add the garlic and jalapeño pepper and toss to cook for 2 minutes. Remove the pepper mixture and transfer to a plate. Add 1 tablespoon (15 ml) of olive oil to the hot wok. Add the calamari and toss to cook for 1 minute, remove, and transfer to a plate. To the wok add the wine, balsamic vinegar, lemon juice, and lemon zest, and stir to combine and heat through. Add the pepper-onion mixture back to the hot wok. Toss with the thyme, basil, parsley, pepper flakes, and mango. Add the calamari and toss to combine and heat through. Serve in shallow appetizer bowls with grilled ciabatta bread, or with sticky rice for an entree.

chapter 4

Cast-Iron Griddle, Grill, and Pizza Pan Cooking

Grill-Pan Panini—Five Delicious Recipes

Panini are quite easy to make. The key to fast panini making is to have all your ingredients prepared and in front of you. Cast-iron grill pans are perfect for panini sandwiches, with little cleanup after the fact. Most recently available are panini presses that come with some popular grill pans. If you are able to find this set, heat the grill pan over medium heat with the press in it, remove the press, add the panini, and top with the hot press to cook. If you can't find a panini press, simply use a heavy cast-iron skillet to press the panini in the pan. Or to be even more rustic, wrap a heavy brick with foil and use it as your "Old World" press.

Unique ways of indoor cooking are growing in popularity, and stovetop grilling is no exception. More popular than ever is grilling on a cast-iron stovetop grill pan or griddle. Probably most recognizable among the cast-iron griddles are the rectangular-shaped, gridiron griddles. Flat on one side and ribbed on the other, these pans allow for cooking ample food with or without grill marks. The versatility of cast-iron grill pans and griddles is endless, producing everything from kebabs, steaks, and hamburgers to panini and complete breakfast meals. These griddles and grill pans are a must-have in any kitchen.

Panini sandwiches have also hit the culinary scene with a vengeance, as have the many electric panini grills on which to cook them. Forget about all the necessary counter space and cords and reach instead for your trusty cast-iron grill pan with a grill press. Use it to cook panini like a professional with beautiful, deep grill marks and a crisp, toasted crust.

Right along with the popularity of cast-iron grill pans are cast-iron pizza pans. With the same effect as a pizza stone, cast-iron pizza pans conduct heat evenly and intensely, creating a delicious crunchy, toasted crust. Found in 14" (35 cm) diameter, the pizza pans are also great for quesadillas and biscuits, as well as for other cooking applications. All of these cast-iron products are cared for the same as you would any cast-iron pan (see the cleaning and care instructions on page 12) and can last forever.

Panini **Cubano**

Cubano sandwiches, brought to the States in the early 1800s, are quite popular in Florida, where the Cuban culture is alive and kicking. Typically a combination of roast pork, ham, a spicy mustard mixture, and pickles, Cubano sandwiches should be enjoyed on Cuban bread. If this isn't available in your area, then a Portuguese roll or soft Italian roll will do.

2 tablespoons (28 g)
unsalted butter, softened

4 Cuban rolls,
Portuguese rolls, or
soft Italian rolls

1 1/2 tablespoons (22 g)
mayonnaise

2 teaspoons (10 g) Dijon mustard

4 slices deli Swiss cheese

1/2 pound (225 g) roasted
pork loin, thinly sliced

1/2 pound (225 g) deli ham, sliced

16 slices dill pickle

Preheat a well-seasoned, cast-iron stovetop grill pan with a panini press over medium-high heat. Cut sandwich rolls in half horizontally. Brush the outsides of each slice with softened butter. In a small bowl, combine the mayonnaise with the Dijon mustard. Spread the cut side of each roll half with one-quarter of the mayonnaise mixture. Place one slice of the Swiss cheese on each roll half. Place one-quarter of the sliced roasted pork loin, one-quarter of the ham, and four pickle slices on one roll half and top with the other roll half. Place on a hot grill pan, pressing with a panini press or a heavy skillet. Turn to grill the other side if necessary.

Black Forest Ham and Gruyère Panini

The sweetness of caramelized onions adds a delicious flavor to this combination of Black Forest ham and Gruyère cheese. Soften your butter and combine with Gorgonzola cheese ahead of time so the flavors have time to intensify.

In a well-seasoned cast-iron skillet heat 2 tablespoons (28 g) of the butter over medium-high heat. Add the onion and cook for 2 minutes, turning, until tender. Reduce heat to low, sprinkle onion with sugar, salt, and black pepper, and cook for 20 minutes, stirring occasionally, until well caramelized. Remove from heat and toss with tarragon and parsley; set aside to cool. Using 2 tablespoons (28 g) of softened butter, brush the outsides of each roll half with butter. Using a fork, combine the remaining 2 tablespoons (28 g) of softened butter with the Gorgonzola cheese into a smooth spread. Spread the insides of each roll half with the Gorgonzola spread. Add caramelized onion mixture to each sandwich, dividing evenly. Top each with one-quarter of the ham, then layer with the Gruyère cheese. Top with remaining roll half and place on hot grill pan. Press with hot panini press, cooking on both sides for 7 minutes, until the cheese is melted. Remove and serve hot.

2 red onions, thinly sliced

2 tablespoons (28 g) unsalted butter, plus 4 tablespoons (55 g) softened

1 tablespoon (4 g) chopped fresh tarragon

1 tablespoon (4 g) chopped fresh flat-leaf parsley

1 teaspoon (4 g) sugar

$^{1}/_{2}$ teaspoon (3 g) salt

$^{1}/_{2}$ teaspoon (1 g) coarsely ground black pepper

4 tablespoons (30 g) crumbled Gorgonzola cheese, softened

4 crusty Italian rolls, sliced in half horizontally

1 pound (455 g) Black Forest ham, thinly sliced

8 slices Gruyère cheese

[Makes 4 panini]

Roasted Chicken and Peach Panini with Prosciutto

In this tasty panini, the classic pairing of prosciutto and melon is trumped by the delicious match of peach and prosciutto with roasted chicken.

2 firm, ripe peaches, peeled, pitted, and cut into 1/2" (1.2 cm) slices

8 slices ciabatta or other crusty Italian bread, cut into 1/2" (12.5 mm) -thick slices

2 tablespoons (28 g) unsalted butter, softened

4 tablespoons (80 g) peach preserves

1/2 cup (75 g) crumbled goat cheese

1 pound (455 g) roasted deli chicken, thinly sliced

8 thin slices prosciutto

1 cup (60 g) watercress, divided

Preheat a well-seasoned, cast-iron grill pan over medium heat. Place the peach slices on the grill pan and cook until grill marks appear, about 2 minutes per side. Transfer to a plate and set aside. Brush one side of each bread slice with melted butter. Lay the slices buttered side down on a clean, dry work surface. Spread the insides of four slices with peach preserves. Sprinkle the goat cheese over the top. Working on the other four slices of bread, divide the prosciutto and chicken among them, topping with watercress. Close the sandwiches. Place on the hot grill pan and press with the panini press. Grill until the sandwich is warmed through and the jam begins to run, about 5 minutes per side. Cut in half diagonally and serve.

[Makes 4 panini]

BST Panini with Fontina

Tender, young, baby spinach puts the S in the BST. The leaves hold up to the heat of the grill pan, giving a bit of a twist to a classic.

4 tablespoons (63 g) mayonnaise

1 tablespoon (3 g) chopped green olives

1 tablespoon (1.5 g) chopped sun-dried tomatoes

Salt and freshly ground black pepper

8 slices sourdough bread, cut 1/2" (12.5 mm) thick

2 tablespoons (28 g) butter, softened

4 ounces (55 g) Fontina cheese, thinly sliced

1 cup (20 g) baby spinach leaves, washed and dried

8 slices smoked bacon, cooked

1 large heirloom tomato, thinly sliced

In a small bowl stir together the mayonnaise, green olives, and sun-dried tomatoes. Season with salt and black pepper, stir, and set aside. Preheat a cast-iron grill pan with panini press over medium heat. Brush one side of each bread slice with softened butter. Lay each slice, buttered side down, on a flat surface. Spread each bread slice with the mayonnaise mixture. Working on four bread slices, begin layering ingredients, first with half the Fontina cheese divided among the four, topping that with spinach, then bacon, then tomato, and finishing with the remaining cheese. Top with remaining bread. Place each sandwich in the hot grill pan, topping with the panini press, and cook until the cheese melts, about 7 minutes on each side.

Roasted Peppercorn Turkey with Bacon, Provolone, and Avocado Panini

I am a huge fan of fresh avocado and think that it simply makes a sandwich better. Whether served hot or cold, avocado is a great complement to the turkey and bacon in this easy-to-prepare panini.

½ cup (112 g) mayonnaise

1 tablespoon (8 g) sour cream

1 teaspoon (5 ml) chopped chipotle chile in adobo

1 teaspoon (5 ml) lime juice

½ teaspoon (1.25 g) lime zest

1 tablespoon (4 g) chopped fresh cilantro

2 tablespoons (28 g) butter, softened

8 thick slices whole wheat or multigrain bread

8 slices provolone cheese

1 pound (455 g) deli peppercorn turkey breast, thinly sliced

8 slices smoked bacon, cooked

1 ripe avocado, peeled, pitted, and cut in ¼" (6 mm) slices

In a small bowl stir together the mayonnaise, sour cream, chipotle pepper, lime juice, lime zest, and cilantro. Preheat a well-seasoned, cast-iron grill pan with a panini press over medium heat. Spread one side of each bread slice with softened butter. Lay the bread slices on a clean work surface, buttered side down. Spread each bread slice with mayonnaise mixture and add one slice of provolone cheese to each. Working on four of the slices, divide the turkey breast among them, topping each with two slices of bacon. Close the sandwiches with the remaining cheese-topped bread slices. Grill, pressing with a panini press or heavy skillet, until the cheese is melted, about 5 minutes on each side. Remove the panini from the grill pan and pull apart, adding the sliced avocado in the middle, then push back together, slice, and serve.

Rustic Berry Skillet Galette with Almonds

A galette is a rustic, folded tart piled high with ingredients, usually mixed fruits and berries.
I have paired fresh, ripe blackberries, blueberries, and raspberries with strawberries to create a sweet and tart pastry.

1/2 pint (110 g) raspberries

1/2 pint (110 g) golden raspberries

1 pint (220 g) strawberries, hulled and sliced

1 pint (220 g) blueberries

1/3 cup (50 g) brown sugar

1 1/2 teaspoons (3.75 g) grated orange zest

1 teaspoon (2.5 g) grated lemon zest

1 teaspoon (5 ml) vanilla extract

2 tablespoons (28 ml) heavy cream

1/4 cup (30 g) sliced almonds, toasted and chopped

1 recipe Pastry Dough (recipe follows), or one store-bought 12" (30 cm) round pastry dough

FOR PASTRY DOUGH:
Makes enough dough for 1 single-crust pie, tart, or galette

1 1/4 cups (140 g) all-purpose flour

1 tablespoon (12 g) sugar

1/2 teaspoon (3 g) salt

1/4 cup (55 g) cold unsalted butter, cut into 3/4" (18 mm) pieces

3 tablespoons (40 g) cold vegetable shortening, cut into 3/4" (18 mm) pieces

3 tablespoons (42 ml) ice water

[For the pastry dough]
To make the dough in a food processor, combine the flour, sugar, and salt in the bowl of the food processor fitted with the blade attachment. Pulse to combine, add the pieces of the butter and shortening, and pulse until reduced to ½" (12.5 mm) pieces. Add the water a little at a time and pulse until the dough just begins to come together. Remove the dough to a work surface and shape into a 12" (30 cm) disk. Wrap in plastic wrap and refrigerate until well chilled, at least 2 hours.

Preheat oven to 400°F (200°C, or gas mark 6). Working on a clean, dry, flat surface, dust the surface of the baking sheet and rolling pin with flour, roll out chilled pastry dough into a 13" (32.5 cm) round about ⅛" (3 mm) thick. Lift and turn the dough as necessary and dust the surface and rolling pin with flour as needed to prevent sticking. Cover with plastic wrap and set aside.

In a large bowl toss the berries with sugar, zests, and vanilla extract. Uncover dough and transfer to a well-seasoned cast-iron griddle pan or oiled pizza pan. Pile berry mixture in the center of the dough, leaving a 3" (7.5 cm) border uncovered. Fold the dough up and over the berries, pleating the folds, leaving the berries exposed in the center. Brush the dough with cream, sprinkle with chopped almonds, and bake for 40 minutes. Remove, let cool for 5 minutes, slice, and serve.

If making for later use, bake, cool, and cover with plastic wrap, then refrigerate until ready to serve. To serve, preheat the oven to 300°F (150°C, or gas mark 2). Remove the galette from the refrigerator, uncover, and warm in the oven for 15 minutes. It may be necessary to cover with aluminum foil to prevent overbrowning of the pastry dough.

[Makes 4 sandwiches]

Grilled **Lamb Kebabs with Feta Orzo**

Lamb is a delicious meat that isn't always the first thought for dinner. Tender with a mild but unique flavor, it is perfect for kebabs. This entire dish may be prepared ahead of time as a time saver, taking only a few minutes in the grill pan to grill the kebabs.

¾ cup (185 g) plain yogurt

1 pound (455 g) lamb cut from the loin, shoulder, or leg, trimmed and cut into 1" (2.5 cm) cubes

1 tablespoon (7 g) paprika

½ teaspoon (3 g) salt

1 teaspoon (2 g) freshly ground black pepper

3 tablespoons (42 ml) olive oil

2 tablespoons (14 g) sour cream

¼ cup (25 g) English cucumber, peeled, seeded, and minced

3 tablespoons (12 g) minced fresh mint

2 tablespoons (28 ml) lemon juice

1 teaspoon (2.5 g) lemon zest

Feta Creamed Orzo (recipe follows)

FOR FETA CREAMED ORZO:

1 pound (2.2 kg) dried orzo

½ cup (120 ml) heavy cream

8 ounces (150 g) feta cheese, crumbled, plus ¼ cup (38 g) for garnish

Salt and black pepper

2 tablespoons (7.5 g) chopped fresh flat-leaf parsley

Line a fine sieve with cheesecloth and place over a bowl, add the yogurt, cover, and refrigerate for 2 hours to drain. Toss the lamb with 2 tablespoons (28 ml) of the olive oil, paprika, salt, and black pepper. Run the lamb on bamboo skewers (presoaked according to package directions) cut to a length to fit in your stovetop grill pan, cover, and refrigerate for at least 30 minutes or up to overnight.

Remove the yogurt from the refrigerator and discard the bowl drippings. In a small bowl mix together the drained yogurt, the 1 remaining tablespoon (14 ml) of olive oil, sour cream, cucumber, mint, lemon juice, and lemon zest. Preheat a well-seasoned, cast-iron grill pan over medium-high heat. Place the kebabs on the grill pan and cook for 12 minutes, turning after 6 minutes, to grill all sides. Place the orzo on a platter and top with the kebabs, drizzling with the cucumber-yogurt sauce.

[For Feta Creamed Orzo]
Bring a large pot of salted water to a boil. Add the orzo and cook until al dente, 9 minutes. Remove, drain, and wash under cold water. Return the orzo to the cooking pot and add the heavy cream and feta cheese. Stir constantly over medium heat to melt the feta cheese into the cream; season with salt and black pepper. Remove from heat, stir in parsley, and serve with a sprinkling of additional crumbled feta cheese.

Grilled **Cornflake-Crusted French Toast**

One of my favorite breakfast meals is stuffed French toast. I just got tired of the same old thing, so I began coating it with the crunch of cornflake cereal and created a new breakfast favorite. Lightly coated with cornflakes and cooked on a griddle, this stuffed French toast has a place at any breakfast table.

4 large eggs

1 tablespoon (12 g) granulated sugar, divided

1/2 teaspoon (2.5 ml) vanilla extract

pinch of salt

1 cup (235 ml) half-and-half

2 cups (230 g) crushed cornflake cereal

8 slices thin, day-old white sandwich bread

4 tablespoons (80 g) fig preserves

2 tablespoons (14 g) cream cheese

2 very ripe bananas, thinly sliced

In a large bowl whisk together the eggs, 1 tablespoon (12 g) of the sugar, vanilla extract, salt, and half-and-half. Place the crushed cereal in a shallow dish. In a small bowl combine the fig preserves with the cream cheese, using a fork. Place four slices of the bread on a flat, dry work surface, spreading each with 2 teaspoons of the preserve mixture. Top with a few slices of the banana and then the remaining bread to form a sandwich, pressing to tightly close.

Preheat oven to 350°F (180°C, or gas mark 4). Heat a well-seasoned, cast-iron griddle over medium heat with butter or oil. Place one sandwich in the batter, coating well. Remove and place in the crushed cereal, pressing to coat each side with crumbs. Place on hot griddle, cooking for 4 minutes per side, until golden brown. Remove, place all on a baking sheet, and bake until cooked through, about 8 minutes. Remove, slice each in half diagonally, and serve immediately with butter and syrup.

Cast Iron Cooking

Grilled **Portobello and Provolone Beef Burgers**

With the evolution of stovetop grill pans, indoor grilling is possible, and our favorite summer dishes can now be prepared and enjoyed all year long with ease. Hamburgers, possibly the favorite summertime meal, offer limitless possibilities. Here, I have married the ground sirloin with the hearty flavors of portobello mushrooms and provolone cheese.

2 pounds (1 kg) good-quality ground angus beef

1 cup (100 g) chopped fresh portobello mushrooms

$1/2$ cup (50 g) chopped Provolone cheese

$1^1/2$ teaspoons (4.5 g) ancho chile powder or Mexican chile powder

1 teaspoon (3 g) garlic powder

$1/2$ teaspoon (3 g) salt

$1/2$ teaspoon (1 g) freshly ground black pepper

2 dashes hot sauce

6 seeded hamburger buns, sliced in half

6 slices deli cheddar cheese

12 slices cooked bacon, optional

In a large bowl, combine the ground beef with the mushroom, provolone cheese, chile powder, garlic powder, salt, black pepper, and hot sauce. Using your hands, combine the flavors thoroughly. Form the meat mixture into eight 1" (2.5 cm) thick patties, cover with plastic wrap, and refrigerate until ready to cook and serve.

Preheat a well-seasoned, cast-iron grill pan over medium-high heat. Preheat the oven broiler to high heat and place an oven rack in the lower third of the oven. Spray the burgers and grill pan with nonstick cooking spray. Place the burgers on the grill pan (in batches if necessary) and grill for about 10 minutes per side for medium or 15 minutes per side for well done. Top with cheddar cheese and place under the broiler to melt. Place each bun, cut side up, on a baking tray and spray with vegetable oil; place under the broiler to toast. Serve each burger with condiments and toppings, including bacon, if desired.

[Serves 4]

Heirloom Tomato, Bacon, and Basil Pizza

Heirloom tomatoes not only add ripe, fresh flavor to a pizza but make for a gorgeous presentation. The variety of color, texture, and size allow for an artful arrangement as a pizza topping. Whatever medley of heirlooms you can find for this garden-fresh summer delight will create a zesty palette.

3 tablespoons (42 ml) extra-virgin olive oil

3 cloves garlic, minced

3 anchovy fillets

1 recipe Neapolitan Pizza dough (recipe page 86)

1/4 cup (20 g) shredded fresh Parmigiano-Reggiano cheese

8 ounces (112 g) shredded low-moisture mozzarella cheese

4 slices thick-cut bacon, chopped, fried crisp, and drained

1/2 pound (225 g) assorted heirloom tomatoes, thinly sliced

8 large, fresh basil leaves, roughly torn

Freshly ground black pepper

In a small skillet heat the olive oil over medium-high heat. Add the garlic and anchovy fillets and cook for 3 minutes, until the anchovies have practically dissolved; set aside. Using a rolling pan or your hands, either roll or stretch the pizza dough to fit a 16" (40 cm) cast-iron pizza pan. Place the dough on the pan, brushing with the anchovy oil mixture. Sprinkle the dough evenly with the Parmigiano-Reggiano and mozzarella cheese; top evenly with bacon and then tomatoes. Sprinkle tomatoes with basil and season with black pepper. Bake on the center rack of the hot oven for 20 to 25 minutes, until the crust begins to brown around the edges and the cheese is melted and bubbling. Remove and let rest for 5 minutes, then slice and serve.

Breakfast Johnnycakes **with Plums and Blackberries**

Johnnycakes, believed to have arrived on the culinary scene before pancakes, were foreign to me until I moved to New England in 1992. Johnnycakes are the denser, cornmeal version of pancakes and are often served as a savory accompaniment to appetizers or dinner.
I enjoy the thick, dense texture of johnnycakes sweetened, as a breakfast alternative.

1 cup (110 g) all-purpose flour

1 teaspoon (1.5 g) baking soda

2 teaspoons (3 g) baking powder

2 1/2 tablespoons (37 g) sugar

1/4 teaspoon (.5 g) ground nutmeg

1/2 teaspoon (3 g) salt

1–1 1/2 cups (235–355 ml) milk

3/4 cup (100 g) finely ground yellow cornmeal

6 tablespoons (83 g) unsalted butter, melted, or bacon grease

2 eggs, lightly beaten

1/2 cup (62.5 g) chopped, toasted pecans

1/2 cup (55 g) halved blackberries

1 cup (225 g) peeled, thinly sliced plums

In a large bowl combine the flour, baking soda, baking powder, sugar, salt, and nutmeg, stirring with a whisk. In a small saucepan over medium-high heat, warm the milk until just beginning to bubble around the edges. Remove from the heat and set aside 1/2 cup (120 ml) of the milk. Using a whisk, stir the cornmeal into the milk remaining in the saucepan, cover, and set aside for 10 minutes. Add the butter and eggs to the saucepan, stirring to combine. Add the cornmeal mixture to the flour mixture, stirring to combine, then add up to 1/2 cup (120 ml) of the reserved hot milk if the batter appears too thick (note, however, that it should be thicker than a traditional pancake batter). Gently fold in the blackberry halves and pecans and let rest for 10 minutes.

Heat a well-seasoned and oiled cast-iron griddle over medium heat, spread with butter or bacon grease, and heat. Scoop 1/4 cup (60 ml) portions of batter onto the hot griddle and add 2 or 3 plum slices to each. Cook until golden brown, about 2 to 3 minutes. Flip and cook for an additional 2 or 3 minutes, remove and serve immediately with butter and maple syrup.

[Serves 4]

Pesto and Black Olive Pizza

In New York City, just about every pizza joint serves a version of this classic combination. Traditionally, black olives are preferred, but experiment with your favorite olive if you like.

1 recipe Neapolitan-style Pizza Dough (recipe follows)

1 cup (260 g) basil pesto

8 ounces (225 g) fresh buffalo mozzarella cheese, sliced into large pieces

1 (4-ounce [115 g]) can sliced black olives

2 tablespoons (14 g) grated parmesan cheese

Preheat oven to 450°F (230°C, or gas mark 8). Stretch dough to fit a 16" (40 cm) cast-iron pizza pan. Spread pesto over dough in an even layer. Distribute sliced mozzarella cheese evenly on the dough. Top with sliced olives and sprinkle with Parmesan cheese. Place pizza on the center rack of the hot oven. Bake until golden and bubbling, about 20 minutes. Remove and let rest for 5 minutes, slice, and serve.

Neapolitan-Style Pizza Dough

The Neapolitan method of making pizza is widely regarded as the "true" style, even considered by some to be the best in the world. This dough gives the best combination of ingredients indicative to a genuine Neapolitan-style dough.

1 cup warm water (110–115°F [43–46°C])

1 (1/4-ounce [7.5-g]) packet active dry yeast

2 cups (220 g) all-purpose flour

1 cup (110 g) cake flour (not self-rising)

1 1/2 teaspoon (3 g) salt

Olive oil for brushing bowl

Combine the water and yeast in a large bowl and stir until dissolved. Combine the flours in a mixing bowl, using a whisk to stir. In a separate mixing bowl combine 2 cups (220 g) of the flour mixture with the salt, make a well in the center. Pour the yeast mixture into the well and begin to incorporate the flour, pulling from the sides with a wooden spoon and stirring until it all comes together. If it becomes too sticky to handle, add an additional 1/2 cup (55 g) of flour and incorporate. Turn the dough out onto a lightly floured

surface and incorporate the remaining ½ to 1 cup (55 to 110 g) of flour, kneading and working the dough. To knead the dough, use the heel of your hand to push the dough down and away from you. Give the dough a one-quarter turn, again fold the sides in and push down and away with the heel of your hand. Repeat this process, pulling in the flour gradually and working it into the dough. Knead the dough until smooth and form into a ball.

Coat a large mixing bowl with olive oil, place the dough ball in the bowl, turn to coat with oil, cover with plastic wrap, and place in a warm, draft-free area to rise, until double its original size. (If you aren't planning to use the dough immediately, form it into two separate balls, rub with oil, place in plastic bags, and refrigerate overnight. This extended rising time will allow the flavors of the dough to intensify as the yeast takes longer to activate. When ready to use, bring to room temperature and then let rise in a warm, draft-free place.) Punch down the risen dough and divide in half, then use as directed. At this point, too, the dough can be placed in plastic bags and refrigerated. If using the refrigeration method, remove and bring to room temperature before proceeding. Dough can be frozen as well; after kneading the first time, place in freezer bags or containers and freeze for up to 3 months. When ready to use, thaw at room temperature or refrigerated, allow to rise double the original size, punch down, and using according to recipe directions.

[Serves 6]

Grilled **Red Snapper with English Pea Puree and Heirloom Tomato Salad**

This dish requires several steps to complete but is a great dinner party treat. The layers of flavors and textures will wow your guests with the succulent, flaky finish of the grilled snapper.

FOR THE CUCUMBER WATER:
Makes about ¹/₃ cup (80 ml)

2 cucumbers (about 1 pound [455 g]), peeled and chopped

1 (¹/₄ pound [115 g]) heirloom tomato, chopped

1 tablespoon (4 g) chopped fresh mint

¹/₄ teaspoon (1.5 g) salt

FOR THE TOMATO SALAD:

1 navel orange

1 pound (455 g) assorted heirloom tomatoes, chopped

¹/₄ cup (15 g) loosely packed watercress leaves

2 tablespoons (7.5 g) thinly sliced fresh basil

1 tablespoon (15 ml) extra-virgin olive oil

2 teaspoons (2 g) finely chopped fresh chives

1 teaspoon (2.5 g) finely chopped fresh lemon thyme

¹/₄ teaspoon (.5 g) black pepper

¹/₄ teaspoon (2 g) sugar

¹/₄ teaspoon (1.5 g) salt

FOR THE PEA PUREE:
Makes about 1¹/₂ cups (338 g)

1 tablespoon (14 g) butter

¹/₄ cup (40 g) finely chopped shallots

1 teaspoon (3 g) minced garlic

1 cup (150 g) blanched English peas

¹/₂ cup (120 ml) vegetable stock

¹/₄ cup (120 ml) heavy cream

8 leaves fresh mint

¹/₄ teaspoon (1.5 g) salt

¹/₈ teaspoon (.25 g) black pepper

FOR THE FISH:

6 (5- to 7-ounce [140- to 196-g]) red snapper or sea bass fillets

Salt and freshly cracked black pepper, to taste

[For cucumber water]

Puree cucumber, tomato, mint, and salt in a blender until smooth, about 30 seconds. Line a fine-mesh sieve with a dampened paper towel or cheesecloth and set over a large glass measure. Transfer the cucumber puree to the sieve and let drain until all the liquid has run through, about 20 minutes, which should yield about ⅔ cup (160 ml). Squeeze out paper towel to gain more liquid. Transfer liquid to a saucepan and boil until reduced to about ⅓ cup (80 ml). Remove from heat and cool to room temperature.

[For heirloom tomato salad]

Segment the orange by peeling away the peel, including the white pith. Cut segments over a bowl to collect the juice. Toss the orange segments and juice with the remaining tomato salad ingredients. Stir in the cooled cucumber water.

[For pea puree]

Melt the butter in a small saucepan over medium-high heat. Add the shallots and cook for 3 minutes. Add the garlic and cook for about 1 minute. Add the English peas and cook, stirring frequently, for 3 minutes. Add the vegetable stock and bring the liquid to a boil. Reduce heat to a simmer and cook for 10 minutes.

Remove from the heat and transfer the peas and liquid to a blender. Add the heavy cream, mint, salt, and pepper, and blend, on low speed, for 1 to 2 minutes, or until the peas form a smooth puree. Be careful while blending the hot ingredients: make sure to hold the lid securely with a thick kitchen towel. Return the puree to the saucepan and keep warm.

[For fish]

Heat a well-seasoned, 10" cast-iron grill pan over medium-high heat and spray with nonstick cooking spray or coat generously with vegetable oil. Season fish with salt and pepper and grill the fish fillets until browned on both sides, about 7 minutes per side, until the fish is flaky. Place a mound of pea puree on each plate, top with a fish fillet, and finish with a scoop of tomato salad.

Black Dog Banana-Blueberry Pancakes

Since 1971, Martha's Vineyard has been home to the Black Dog Tavern. Opened originally as a year-round eatery for island natives, the Black Dog is now every summer visitor's first stop on their trip to the vineyard. Patrons wait in line for hours to enjoy a Black Dog breakfast, many of which consist of the tavern's delicious banana-blueberry pancakes. Not inclined to compete with a delicious breakfast original, I offer you the Black Dog's one-and-only.

3/4 cup (85 g) unbleached all-purpose flour

1/4 cup (27 g) buckwheat flour

1/4 cup (27 g) whole wheat flour

2 tablespoons (18 g) cornmeal (optional)

1 tablespoon (12 g) sugar

1 1/2 teaspoons (2.25 g) baking powder

1/2 teaspoon (0.75 g) baking soda

1/2 teaspoon (3 g) salt

1 1/2 teaspoons (3.5 g) cinnamon

2 eggs

2 tablespoons (28 g) melted butter

1 to 1 1/2 cups (235–355 ml) whole milk

1 cup (110 g) fresh blueberries

1 banana, thinly sliced

In a medium bowl, mix together the dry ingredients. In a separate bowl beat the eggs with 1 cup (235 ml) of milk and the melted butter. Add the wet mixture to the dry, mixing until a thin batter is formed. Add up to 1/2 cup (120 ml) of milk if the mixture is too thick, being careful not to stir too much. When the batter is the right consistency (similar to that of cake batter), gently fold in the blueberries. Heat a well-seasoned, oiled, cast-iron griddle over medium heat. Ladle a 5" (13 cm) circle of batter onto the griddle. Drop a few slices of banana into each circle. Cook pancakes until the tops are covered with tiny bubbles, then flip them over and finish cooking. Serve hot, with butter and maple syrup.

Cast-Iron Roasting, Braising, and Baking

Old-Fashioned Versatility

For this chapter I have created recipes that utilize roasting pans, braising pans, and bakeware, all available in traditional black or enamel-coated cast iron, having the same great effect on cooking as classic skillets. From Braised Short Ribs to Cherry Clafouti, cast-iron bakeware, including casseroles, braising pans, drop biscuit pans, and muffin pans, doesn't have to be limited to the more recognizable skillets and griddles. Muffin pans and drop biscuit pans are the quickest way to achieve old-fashioned greatness in the kitchen.

Roasting pans that feed a crowd and biscuit pans that dish out individually baked servings are as versatile as they are functional. A favorite pan of mine, the five-quart (about five-liter) buffet casserole, is perfect for braising and roasting because it is transferred easily from the stovetop to the oven. From Pepper Jelly–Braised Short Ribs to Whole Roasted Teriyaki-Orange Chicken, the buffet casserole pan gives an attractive presentation. For years, cornbread has been baked in oddly shaped cast iron pans, and here I have explored new uses for these pans in such recipes as Cherry-Apricot Clafouti and Gingerbread Cupcakes with Gingered Apricot Glaze.

Gingerbread Cupcakes with Gingered Apricot Glaze

Autumn, for me, evokes feelings of home-cooked meals prepared in cast iron. Nothing welcomes the fall like the smell of baking gingerbread. Baking this batter in a well-seasoned, cast-iron muffin dish develops a crisp outer layer to the muffins. Break them open quickly once they're out of the oven, rubbing with butter on the inside.

2 cups (220 g) all-purpose flour	1 egg	FOR APRICOT GLAZE:
1 teaspoon (1.5 g) baking soda	$^{1}/_{2}$ cup (170 g) light molasses	$1^{1}/_{2}$ cups (480 g) apricot preserves
1 tablespoon (7 g) ground ginger	1 tablespoon (6 g) minced crystallized ginger	3 tablespoons (42 ml) water
2 teaspoons (4.6 g) ground cinnamon	1 cup (200 g) sugar	2 tablespoons (12 g) minced crystallized ginger
$^{1}/_{2}$ teaspoon (1.25 g) ground cloves	$^{1}/_{2}$ cup (112 g) unsalted butter, melted	$^{1}/_{2}$ teaspoon (1.25 g) ground ginger
$^{1}/_{2}$ teaspoon (1.25 g) ground allspice	1 cup (235 ml) buttermilk	$^{1}/_{2}$ teaspoon (1.25 g) ground cinnamon
	1 cup (140 g) whipped cream or vanilla ice cream, to serve	

Lightly butter well-seasoned cast-iron muffin pans or a 10" (25 cm) cast-iron skillet or a 9" x 13" (22.5 x 32.5 cm) cast-iron cake pan. Preheat the oven to 350°F (180°C, or gas mark 4). In a large bowl sift together the dry ingredients. In the bowl of an electric mixer fitted with the paddle attachment, beat the egg, molasses, crystallized ginger, sugar, and melted butter until thick. Gradually mix in the dry ingredients, alternating with the buttermilk. Beat for 1 minute after each addition to combine the ingredients well. Pour the batter into each muffin cup or into the buttered skillet. Top each muffin with a slice of apricot or, if using the skillet, place twelve slices evenly dispersed in a concentric circle around the perimeter of the skillet. Bake for 35 to 40 minutes, until a wooden skewer inserted in the middle comes out clean.

Meanwhile prepare the apricot glaze: combine all the ingredients in a saucepan and place over medium heat. Bring to a boil, stirring occasionally, then reduce the heat to low, keeping warm until ready to use.

Remove the muffins from the oven and let cool completely before removing. Serve, drizzled with Apricot Glaze and whipped cream or vanilla ice cream.

Pepper Jelly–Braised Short Ribs

If you have a while to keep something in the oven for dinner, short ribs are the way to go. They are so tender and juicy, and the meat just falls from the bone. For a barbecue-inspired meal without the fuss of a charcoal grill, braised short ribs are the answer. Don't be alarmed by the list of ingredients; the end result is well worth the prep time.

³/₄ cup (85 g) all-purpose flour

¹/₄ cup (34 g) finely ground yellow cornmeal or masa harina

1 tablespoon (10 g) packed dark brown sugar

1 teaspoon (2.3 g) ground cumin

1 teaspoon (2.3 g) ground coriander

1 teaspoon (2.3 g) ground mustard

¹/₄ teaspoon (0.5 g) ground cloves

¹/₂ teaspoon (3 g) salt

1 teaspoon (1 g) freshly ground black pepper

2¹/₂ pounds (1 kg) short ribs, trimmed and cut into individual ribs

2 tablespoons (28 ml) olive oil

1 small yellow onion, thinly sliced

8 cloves garlic, coarsely chopped

¹/₂ cup (65 g) chopped carrot

¹/₂ cup (60 g) chopped leeks

¹/₂ cup (55 g) chopped parsnips

2 cups (475 ml) pinot noir

1 cup (150 g) peeled, seeded, and chopped fresh or canned tomatoes

2 quarts (950 ml) beef stock

¹/₂ cup (160 g) jalapeño jelly

2 bay leaves

4 sprigs fresh flat-leaf parsley

2 sprigs fresh thyme

In a medium bowl stir together the flour, cornmeal, brown sugar, cumin, coriander, ground mustard, cloves, salt, and black pepper. Season the ribs thoroughly with the spice mixture, rubbing in well; set aside. Heat the olive oil in a large, well-seasoned cast-iron Dutch oven or braising pan over medium-high heat. When the oil is smoking, add the ribs and brown on all sides, about 7 minutes, turning occasionally. Remove the ribs and set aside. To the pan add the onion, garlic, carrot, leeks, and parsnips, and cook, stirring, for 15 minutes, until browned and somewhat caramelized. Add the wine and deglaze the pan, cooking for 5 minutes, reducing the wine by half. Add the ribs back to the pan with the tomatoes, beef stock, and jalapeño jelly. Stir and bring to a boil, add the bay leaves, parsley, and thyme, cover, and place on the center rack of the hot oven. Cook, covered, for 2½ hours, until the rib meat falls from the bone. Serve hot with sauce and vegetables.

Cherry-Apricot Clafouti

A traditional country French dessert, clafouti
(pronounced kla-foo-tee) has a base layer of
fruit topped with a batter and is served warm,
usually with whipped cream or ice cream.
Traditional clafouti is made with cherries but
any fruit such as peaches, apricots, apples, or
pears can be used. Mixing a combination of
fresh berries is also quite good.

1 tablespoon (14 g) butter	1 cup (110 g) all-purpose flour
4 eggs	1/4 teaspoon (1.5 g) salt
1/3 cup (115 g) honey	1 cup (235 ml) heavy cream
1/2 teaspoon (.25 ml) vanilla extract	3/4 pound (340 g) sweet cherries, pitted and halved
2 tablespoons (28 g) butter, melted	3/4 pound (340 g) fresh apricots, sliced 1/4" (6 mm) thick
1 tablespoon (15 ml) cherry brandy	1/2 cup (100 g) sugar
	Whipped cream or ice cream, to serve

Preheat the oven to 350°F
(180°C, or gas mark 4). Grease
an oval or rectangular 9" x 13"
(22.5 x 32.5-cm) enamel-coated
cast-iron baking dish with the
tablespoon of butter. In a mixing
bowl, whisk the eggs with the
honey and vanilla extract. Stir in
the butter, brandy, flour, and
salt, mixing well. Add the cream
and whisk to a smooth batter.
In a separate mixing bowl
combine the cherries and the
apricots with the sugar, tossing
to coat evenly. Pour the fruit
mixture into the greased dish.
Pour the batter over the fruit,
place in the oven, and bake
for 40 to 45 minutes or until the
cake is firm and spongelike.
Remove from the oven
and cool for 5 minutes before
serving. Serve warm with
whipped cream or your
favorite ice cream.

[Serves 6]

Stuffed Braised Flank Steak

Braising is the technique of searing meat on all sides, sealing in the flavors and moisture, then cooking the meat in the oven for a longer time to tenderize it. Cast iron is perfect for braising because it can be used on the stovetop for searing the meat and then be transferred directly to the oven. Flank steak is best prepared by this method.

4 ounces (38 g, about 2 slices) thickly sliced pancetta, diced

5 tablespoons (150 ml) olive oil

2 shallots, finely chopped

3 large garlic cloves, minced

3/4 cup (85 g) cornbread stuffing mix

1/3 cup (35 g) grated Parmigiano-Reggiano cheese

1/3 cup (50 g) finely chopped Genoa salami

1/4 cup (16 g) chopped fresh flat-leaf parsley

2 tablespoons (7.5 g) chopped fresh oregano, or 1 tablespoon (1.7 g) dried

1 (1 1/2- to 1 3/4-pound [670- to 795-g]) flank steak, butterflied

Salt and freshly ground black pepper, to taste

1 bulb fresh fennel, cleaned, core removed, sliced lengthwise

1 (14-ounce [390-g]) can medium whole black olives

1 pint (300 g) red grape tomatoes

2 sprigs fresh thyme, left whole

6 leaves fresh sage, torn

3 bay leaves

1/4 to 1/2 cup (60–120 ml) beef stock

In a 12" (30 cm) cast-iron skillet over medium-high heat sauté the pancetta, rendering the fat until crisp, about 6 minutes. Transfer the crisp pancetta to paper towels to drain, reserving the fat in the skillet. Add 1 tablespoon (14 ml) of olive oil to the skillet; once hot, add the shallot and sauté for 3 minutes, until translucent. Add the garlic and cornbread stuffing mix, and continue to sauté for an additional 2 minutes. Transfer the mixture to a mixing bowl and set aside to cool. Once cool, add the pancetta, cheese, salami, parsley, and oregano, season with salt and black pepper, mix well, and set aside.

To butterfly the steak, lay flat on a clean, dry surface. Using a long-bladed knife, slice the meat horizontally almost in half, lengthwise, being careful not to cut all the way through the meat (one long edge should remain uncut). Open the meat and press flat. Season both sides of the meat with salt and pepper. Distribute the stuffing mixture evenly across the meat, leaving a 1/2" (12.5 mm) border on all sides. Roll the steak into itself (away from you) into a log. Using kitchen twine, tie the rolled steak, beginning at one end, trussing as you go, and ending at the opposite end. You may need to run one length of twine lengthwise along the log to tie the ends in. Cover and let steak stand for 30 minutes at room temperature, or cover and refrigerate. If refrigerating, remove 30 minutes prior to cooking.

Preheat the oven to 400°F (200°C, or gas mark 6). In a 13 1/4" (33 cm) oval cast-iron skillet (or large round skillet) heat 2 tablespoons (28 ml) of the olive oil over medium-high heat. When hot, place the meat in the skillet, browning on all sides. Once browned on all sides, remove from the skillet. Add the 2 remaining tablespoons (28 ml) of olive oil to the skillet; once hot, add the fennel and black olives and sauté for 4 minutes, until the fennel becomes tender. Add the tomatoes, thyme, sage, and bay leaves to the skillet and toss and sauté for 3 minutes. Add the beef stock to the skillet; return the flank steaks to skillet, laying them on top of vegetable mixture; and place the skillet on the middle rack of the oven. Bake for 45 minutes to an hour, until the internal temperature reads 165°F (74°C) on an instant-read thermometer. Remove, let rest for 10 minutes, slice, and serve. Serve with sautéed vegetables and wild rice.

Whole Roasted Teriyaki-Orange Chicken with Scallions and Green Beans

These days, chicken tends to be sold cut up rather than as a whole bird. I like roasting the bird whole; the technique preserves the natural moisture during cooking, providing juicy and tender meat. If you can find only chicken parts, use what would compose a whole bird. However, if you have access to fresh, whole, farm-raised birds, I encourage their use; you will truly notice the difference.

1 (3^1/$_2$ pound [1.5 kg]) chicken

^{3}/$_4$ cup (185 g) teriyaki sauce

^{1}/$_4$ cup (60 ml) fresh orange juice

^{1}/$_4$ cup (75 g) orange marmalade

2 tablespoons (28 ml) olive oil

6 cloves garlic, thinly sliced

2 bay leaves

2 large pieces orange rind,
white pith removed and trimmed

6 scallions, green parts only,
sliced into large pieces

^{1}/$_2$ pound (225 g) green beans,
ends snipped

Preheat the oven to 375°F (190°C, or gas mark 5). Rinse the chicken and pat dry with paper towels. Tuck the wings under the back and tie the legs together with kitchen twine. In a small bowl combine the teriyaki sauce, orange juice, and orange marmalade. Heat the olive oil in a large cast-iron skillet or Dutch oven over medium-high heat. Add the garlic and sauté for 2 minutes, add the onions and green beans, and cook, stirring, for 4 minutes. Remove from the heat, move the vegetables to the sides of the skillet, add the chicken, and rub thoroughly with the orange-teriyaki sauce. Add the bay leaves and orange rind to the pan, place in the oven, and roast until the juices from under the chicken's leg run clear, about 1 hour, basting every 15 minutes. After 1 hour, turn off the heat and let the chicken rest in the oven with the door cracked open for 15 minutes. Carve and serve with scallions and green beans.

chapter 6

Cast-Iron Dutch Ovens, Fryers, and Kettles

Classic Cast Iron

Dating back to the seventh and eighth centuries, cast-iron pots have played their part in many stages of culinary civilization. Good over an open fire or from stovetop to oven, cast-iron Dutch ovens, fryers, and kettles are a must for every serious cook.

By the sixteenth century, the art of casting iron had become widespread and such cookware had become a valued commodity. Travellers brought much of their original cast iron with them to the New World but quickly began creating and casting additional tools as needed. From the campfires of Lewis and Clark to the chuck wagons of the wild West, cast-iron Dutch ovens and skillets fed the hungry for generations. No matter the weight of the Dutch oven, fryer, or kettle, they were worth their weight in gold because of their durability, cooking capacity, and long-lasting heat.

Bringing this experience to your kitchen is easy with a stovetop, flat-bottomed Dutch oven or fryer. In this chapter, the large capacity of Dutch ovens, fryers, and kettles is vital to the preparation of such dishes as Cast-Iron Texas Chili, Mussels in Lager Broth, and Hot Italian Sausage and Garlic. Looking to fry chicken like our ancestors did? Then cast-iron fryers are your tool—with a deep oil capacity and handled, screened baskets, true chicken frying in cast iron is perfect every time, with even and consistent heating.

Burgundy Beef Stew

A classic in France, Burgundy Beef Stew is the best example of the rich, hearty cooking found in that beautiful wine country. Adapted from a favorite book of mine, *The Perfect Match* by Brian St. Pierre, this stew is rustic in its nature and ideal for cast iron cooking, yet elegant and refined in its heritage. Serve with a bold glass of Burgundy wine.

5 slices bacon, chopped	2 tablespoons (16 g) flour
4 tablespoons (55 g) unsalted butter, divided	3 cups (700 ml) dry red wine
	2 cloves garlic, chopped
8 ounces (225 g) small button mushrooms	1 cup (235 ml) beef broth
4 ounces (115 g) morel mushrooms, chopped	2 sprigs fresh thyme
	2 sprigs fresh sage
16 small white onions, peeled, or 1 cup (130 g) frozen pearl onions, thawed and drained	2 bay leaves
	Salt and freshly ground black pepper, to taste
1 carrot, chopped	2 tablespoons (8 g) chopped fresh parsley
2 pounds (1 kg) beef chuck, cut into 1¹/₂" (12.5 mm) cubes	Boiled potatoes, for serving

Heat a large, well-seasoned cast-iron Dutch oven over medium-high heat. Add the bacon and cook until crisp, then remove the crisp bacon pieces and set aside. Add 2 tablespoons (28 g) of the butter to the bacon fat, stirring to combine and melt. Once the butter is melted, add the mushrooms to the pan, cooking for 3 minutes, until just becoming tender; season with salt and pepper and add the onion and carrot. Continue to cook until the vegetables are tender, about 7 minutes. Using a slotted spoon, transfer the vegetables from the pan to a plate and set aside. Add the remaining 2 tablespoons (28 g) of butter to the hot skillet; once melted, add the beef, tossing and cooking until browned on all sides. Sprinkle the beef with flour and toss in the pan, browning the flour for 3 minutes. Slowly add the red wine to the pan, stirring all the while, scraping up the pan drippings. Bring the wine to a brisk bubble and add the garlic, broth, thyme, sage, and bay leaves. Bring to a boil, reduce heat to a low simmer, cover, and cook for 1 hour. Add the bacon and vegetables back to the pan and season with salt and pepper. Cover and cook for another 30 minutes. Serve garnished with parsley, accompanied with boiled potatoes.

[Serves 4]

Peppercorn Ahi with Smoked Shellfish Bordelaise

For this dish, use only the freshest tuna steaks you can find. The result is tender and succulent tuna with a vibrant burst of flavor in every bite. The smoked seafood in the bordelaise is tremendous. Your local fish market should be able to provide these to you.

4 (6–8 ounce [170- to 225-g]) fresh ahi tuna steaks, cut about 1" (2.5 cm) thick

1 tablespoon (15 ml) olive oil

1 tablespoon (6 g) coarse cracked black pepper

1 tablespoon (6 g) coarsely cracked green peppercorns

1 teaspoon (6 g) kosher salt

FOR THE BORDELAISE:

$1/2$ cup (112 g) cold unsalted butter, cut into tablespoon-size (14 g) pieces

$1/4$ cup (33 g) minced cipollino onions or sweet yellow onion, such as Vidalia

1 teaspoon (3 g) minced fresh garlic

1 pint (455 g) smoked oysters

$1/2$ pound (225 g) smoked shrimp

1 pint (455 g) smoked mussels

$1/2$ pound (225 g) sea scallops

1 teaspoon (2.5 g) chile powder

1 teaspoon (2.5 g) dried oregano

1 teaspoon (2.5 g) paprika

$3/4$ cup (175 g) dry white wine

2 tablespoons (28 ml) cognac or sherry

1 cup (235 ml) fish stock or clam juice

$1/2$ teaspoon (3 g) kosher salt

$1/4$ teaspoon (.5 g) cayenne pepper

1 cup (150 g) peeled, seeded, and diced tomato

$1/4$ cup (25 g) thinly sliced green onion

2 teaspoons (3 g) fresh chopped flat-leaf parsley

2 teaspoons (3 g) fresh chopped tarragon

Place the tuna steaks in a shallow dish or platter and drizzle with olive oil. Coat each steak evenly with a combination of black and green pepper and salt. Cover and refrigerate for 30 minutes. Remove from refrigerator 15 minutes prior to cooking.

In a large, well-seasoned cast-iron Dutch oven, melt 2 tablespoons (28 g) of the butter over medium-high heat.

Add the onion and garlic, and cook until tender, 2 minutes. Add the oysters, shrimp, mussels, and scallops; sprinkle with chile powder, paprika, and oregano, and cook until the scallops become opaque, 3 to 4 minutes. Transfer the seafood to a dish. Add the wine and cognac to the skillet and bring to a boil, cooking to reduce by half. Add the fish stock, salt, and cayenne pepper, and again reduce by

half. Reduce the heat to low, add the tomatoes, and cook for 2 minutes. Whisk in the remaining 6 tablespoons (83 g) of butter, 1 tablespoon at a time, adding the next piece just before the previous has completely melted. Keep the temperature low or the sauce will break. Once all the butter is incorporated, add the green onion, parsley, and tarragon. Add the seafood and any accumulated juices to

the skillet, stir to combine, and cook to heat through. Remove from heat and set aside, keeping warm.

Preheat a stovetop cast-iron grill pan over medium-high heat. Spray with nonstick cooking spray or coat with vegetable oil. Grill each tuna steak for about 4 minutes per side to a pink, rare inside. Serve each steak on top of a ladleful of smoked shellfish bordelaise.

Mussels in Lager Broth

I have probably eaten mussels prepared fifty different ways, all of which have been great — from tomato broth to tomato sauce, white wine and garlic broth, to pinot noir and bacon. I have come up with one that I personally enjoy, especially with a crusty loaf of bread to dip in the delicious broth.

2 tablespoons (28 ml) olive oil

2 medium yellow onions, chopped

6 cloves garlic, minced

1/2 pound (225 g) chorizo, chopped

1 (12-ounce) bottle lager beer

1/2 cup (120 ml) water

3 tablespoons (40 g) butter, at room temperature

2 bay leaves

1 tablespoon (7 g) Old Bay seasoning

1/4 teaspoon (.5 g) crushed red pepper flakes

1 teaspoon (2.5 g) dried oregano

1 tablespoon (6 g) coarsely ground black pepper

2 pounds (1 kg) mussels, cleaned and debearded

Juice of one lemon

In a large Dutch oven heat the oil over medium-high heat, add the onion and garlic, and cook for 7 minutes, until the onion becomes translucent and tender. Add the chorizo, cooking for 3 minutes, stirring occasionally. Add the beer and stir until the foam subsides, then add the water, butter, bay leaves, Old Bay, red pepper flakes, oregano, and black pepper. Stir, bring to a boil, pour in the mussels, and cover to steam for 7 minutes, or until all the mussels are opened. Add a squeeze of lemon juice, toss the mussels in their broth, and serve hot, discarding any unopened mussels.

Fried **Chicken Three Ways**

[Serves 4]

Buttermilk Fried **Chicken**

When developing recipes, I found that the most popular way of preparing fried chicken is by first soaking it for several hours in buttermilk, not only to impart flavor but also to tenderize the meat. In my version, I have added some spice to the soak to better flavor the bird.

2¹/₂ cups (75 ml) buttermilk

2 teaspoons (10 ml) hot sauce

1 tablespoon (18 g) kosher salt

1¹/₂ teaspoons (3 g) ground black pepper

2 tablespoons (18 g) ground dry mustard

1 tablespoon (7 g) paprika

3¹/₂- to 4- pound (1.5- to 2.0-kg) chicken, cut into 8 bone-in serving pieces

2 cups (220 g) all-purpose flour

2 teaspoons (6 g) chile powder

1 teaspoon (3 g) garlic powder

1 teaspoon (3 g) onion powder

¹/₂ teaspoon (3 g) salt

In a large bowl whisk together the buttermilk, salt, pepper, dry mustard, and paprika. Add the chicken pieces, turning to coat, cover, and refrigerate for at least 4 hours or overnight. Remove chicken from refrigerator. In a large, shallow dish mix together the flour, chile powder, garlic powder, and onion powder. Add canola oil to a large, deep cast-iron Dutch oven with a frying basket to a depth of 4" (10 cm), or to a 12" (30 cm) cast-iron skillet to a depth of 1" (2.5 cm).

Heat the oil over medium-high heat to 375°F (190°C, or gas mark 5). Remove the chicken pieces from the buttermilk in batches, letting the excess drain a bit. Dip in the flour mixture, turning to coat evenly and thoroughly, shake off excess, then add to oil. Fry for 12 minutes, turn, and fry for an additional 8 to 10 minutes. Remember that dark meat takes longer than white meat to cook through. Remove the chicken and place on paper towels to drain.

Buttermilk Fried Chicken, this page

Sweet Tea-Soaked Fried Chicken, page 114

Fried Chicken with Onion and Herbs, page 115

Sweet Tea-Soaked
Fried **Chicken**

Another way to prepare fried chicken is by soaking it in a brine—a combination of liquids, salt, and spices that flavor and tenderize the bird. John Fleer, chef at the Inn at Blackberry Farm, in Walland, Tennessee, is considered the creator of this tea-sweetened approach to Southern fried chicken.

1 quart (475 ml) strong brewed tea	3 cups (330 g) all-purpose flour
1 lemon, thinly sliced	2 cups (250 g) masa harina
1 cup (200 g) sugar	2 tablespoons (15 g) Old Bay seasoning
1/2 cup (150 g) kosher salt	1 tablespoon (9 g) chile powder
1 quart (475 ml) ice water	1 teaspoon (6 g) salt
8 chicken leg pieces, separated into drumsticks and thighs	1 teaspoon (2 g) ground black pepper
	8 eggs
	1 cup (235 ml) buttermilk
	Peanut oil for frying

In a large pot combine the tea, lemon, sugar, and kosher salt, and simmer for 5 minutes, or until the salt and sugar dissolve completely. Pour in ice water and cool brine completely. Submerge thighs and drumsticks in brine, cover, and refrigerate for 48 hours. Remove to a wire rack and allow chicken to drain.

In a large bowl, combine 2 cups (220 g) of the flour and the masa harina, Old Bay, chile powder, salt, and pepper. In a medium bowl place remaining 1 cup of flour, and in a third bowl beat eggs with buttermilk. Line up the bowls of flour, egg mixture, and masa harina mixture, in that order. Coat the chicken in the flour, then the egg mixture, then the masa harina mixture, applying pressure to ensure even adherence. Place chicken pieces on a baking sheet and refrigerate for 30 minutes before frying.

Pour oil into a large, well-seasoned cast-iron Dutch oven or fryer to a depth of at least 3" (7.5 cm). Heat the oil to 300°F (150°C, or gas mark 2). Fry the chicken submerged in oil for 15 minutes, or until an instant-read thermometer registers 170°F (77°C) for dark meat, 160°F (72°C) for white meat. (Do not crowd the chicken; you will probably have to do this in about four batches.) Transfer to a rack to drain; serve warm or cold.

[Serves 4]

Fried **Chicken with Onions and Herbs**

A popular way to fry chicken is by seasoning the frying oil. As the herbs begin to blacken, remove them to avoid a bitter flavor. Use herbs with tough stems, such as thyme, rosemary, sage, oregano, or marjoram.

2 pieces each skinless chicken breasts, thighs, drumsticks, and wings

1¹/₂ cups (355 g) buttermilk

1 egg

1 cup (110 g) all-purpose flour

³/₄ cup (105 g) cornmeal

2 cloves garlic, minced

1 tablespoon (4 g) finely minced fresh marjoram or oregano

1 tablespoon (4 g) finely minced fresh basil

1 tablespoon (4 g) finely minced fresh flat-leaf parsley

1 teaspoon (3 g) chile powder

¹/₂ teaspoon (2.5 g) cayenne pepper

1 teaspoon (6 g) salt

1 teaspoon (2 g) freshly cracked black pepper

Peanut oil for frying

2 yellow onions, cut into 1" (2.5 cm) thick slices

6 thick, full sprigs fresh thyme or oregano

2 thick, full sprigs fresh rosemary

2 fresh bay leaves, or 4 dried

Place chicken in a bowl, tossing with 1 cup (235 ml) buttermilk. Cover and refrigerate for at least 1 hour or overnight.

Preheat oven to 400°F (200°C, or gas mark 6). In a shallow bowl, beat egg with a fork until blended, add 1/2 cup (120 ml) of buttermilk, and beat until combined. In a shallow dish, mix the flour, cornmeal, garlic, basil, marjoram, parsley, chile powder, cayenne pepper, salt, and pepper.

Lift the chicken pieces, one at a time, and dip first into the flour mixture, coating evenly, and then into the egg mixture. Dip each piece again into the flour mixture and set aside on a baking sheet. When all pieces are coated, refrigerate uncovered for 15 minutes while the oil heats.

To a well-seasoned cast-iron Dutch oven over high heat add oil to a depth of 4" (10 cm). Heat oil to 350°F (180°oC, or gas mark 4) and add onions, thyme, rosemary, and bay leaves. Working in batches, fry chicken pieces, turning as needed, until well browned on all sides, about 15 minutes, being careful not to crowd the pan. As the pieces are browned, transfer them to two baking sheets, one for white meat and one for dark meat. (Dark meat will take longer to cook than white.) Transfer baking sheets to the oven and bake until cooked through and the juices run clear. Remove chicken pieces as they are done, after 20 to 30 minutes.

Serve immediately, or cool and pack for a picnic.

Lobster Rangoons **over** Mâche Salad with Tarragon-Pomegranate Vinaigrette

Not Asian at all, these appetizers are somewhat of an enigma in culinary history. Their origin is truly unknown. Whatever their lineage, each bite of these little crunchy pleasures is filled with a creamy, flavorful burst.

Peanut oil for frying

1 shallot, minced

2 tablespoons (7.5 g) minced carrot

2 cloves garlic, minced

1 teaspoon (2.7 g)
grated fresh ginger

12 ounces (340 g) lobster meat,
picked over for shells,
finely chopped

1 green onion, finely minced

1 tablespoon (4 g)
finely chopped fresh cilantro

1 tablespoon (4 g)
finely chopped fresh tarragon

4 ounces (115 g)
cream cheese, softened

2 ounces (55 g)
goat cheese, softened

1 teaspoon (5 ml) soy sauce

Juice of 1/2 lemon

1/4 teaspoon (1.5 g) salt

1/4 teaspoon (0.5 g)
freshly ground black pepper

1 (12-ounce [340-g]) package
square wonton wrappers

1 egg white, lightly beaten

Cornstarch for dusting wontons

FOR MÂCHE SALAD:

4 cups (80 g) mixed mâche or
micro greens (or mesclun mix)

1 cup (100 g) shredded English
cucumber, seeded but not peeled

1/4 cup (33 g) shredded red onion

1/2 cup (65 g) toasted pine nuts or
dry roasted peanuts

FOR TARRAGON-POMEGRANATE
VINAIGRETTE:

1/2 cup (120 ml) pomegranate juice

1 teaspoon (2.7 g)
grated fresh ginger

1 teaspoon (2.5 g) lemon zest

1 teaspoon (5 ml) lemon juice

1 tablespoon (15 ml) white
balsamic vinegar or rice vinegar

2 tablespoons (8 g)
chopped fresh tarragon

1 tablespoon (4 g) chopped fresh
chopped flat-leaf parsley

1/4 cup (60 ml) peanut oil

Salt and black pepper, to taste

Heat 1 tablespoon (15 ml) of peanut oil in a deep, well-seasoned cast-iron fryer or wok over medium-high heat. Add the shallot, carrot, garlic, and ginger and cook for 2 minutes, until tender, then remove and set aside to cool. In a large bowl combine the shallot mixture with the lobster meat. Gently fold in the green onion, cilantro, tarragon, cream cheese, goat cheese, soy sauce, lemon juice, salt, and black pepper. Working on a clean, dry, flat work surface, lay out the wonton wrappers and brush with the beaten egg white, getting all the way to the edges. Drop 1 tablespoon of the lobster filling onto the center of each wrapper. Fold each wonton in half, corner to corner, to form a triangle. Press firmly around the edges to seal the wontons. Lightly dust the wontons with cornstarch to prevent sticking, and place on a baking sheet. Heat a 3" (7.5 cm) depth of peanut oil in the cast-iron fryer or wok over medium-high heat to 350°F (180°C, or gas mark 4).

Drop wontons, in batches, into the pot; fry for about 5 minutes, until crisp, turning frequently. Remove with a slotted spoon or strainer and place on a paper towel to drain. Continue frying until all are done. Serve each on top of mâche salad tossed with vinaigrette.

[For Mâche Salad]
Combine salad ingredients in a bowl and toss with Tarragon-Pomegranate Vinaigrette immediately before serving.

[For Tarragon-Pomegranate Vinaigrette]
In a small bowl combine the pomegranate juice with the ginger, lemon zest and juice, balsamic vinegar, tarragon, and parsley. In a slow drizzle, whisk in the peanut oil, creating an emulsion; add more if needed for a thicker vinaigrette. Season with salt and black pepper and refrigerate until ready to use.

Cast-Iron Texas Chili

Cast iron and chili seem created for each other. The history and lore surrounding chili point to Texas as its birthplace. Possibly developed in the late 1600s, the dish is thought to have originally combined the dried meats and crushed chiles available in those times. Today, chilis are as widespread and regionally varied as chowders. Being Texan, I offer a recipe that has the technique and flavor of what is known as Texas chili.

4 slices extra-thick, smoked bacon, chopped

3 medium onions, chopped

10 cloves garlic, minced

4 pounds (1.8kg) boneless beef chuck, trimmed and cut into 1/2" (12.5 mm) cubes

1/3 cup (35 g) chile powder

2 teaspoons (6 g) ancho chile powder

1 tablespoon (7 g) ground cumin

1 teaspoon (2.5 g) cayenne pepper

2 cups (475 ml) water

3 cups (710 g) beef stock

2 teaspoons (5 g) dried oregano

2 teaspoons (12 g) salt

1 tablespoon (12g) sugar

1 tablespoon (10 g) masa harina or finely ground yellow cornmeal

Salt and freshly ground black pepper, to taste

4 dashes hot pepper sauce, such as Tabasco

Sour cream, for garnish

Shredded cheddar cheese, for garnish

Corn tortilla chips, for garnish

2 chopped scallions, for garnish

Heat a large, well-seasoned cast-iron Dutch oven over medium-high heat. Add the bacon and fry until crisp and the fat is rendered. Remove the bacon to drain on paper towels, leaving the remaining hot grease in the pan. Add the onions and garlic to the pan and cook until the onions are tender, about 5 minutes. Add the beef and cook until browned on the outside, about 5 to 6 minutes. Add the chile powders and cumin, stirring well. Add the water and beef stock, enough to cover the mixture, and bring to a simmer. Add the oregano and salt, cover, and simmer for 1½ hours. Add the sugar and masa harina, stirring to combine, allowing to thicken a bit. Add salt, pepper, and hot pepper sauce to season. Cook for an additional 30 minutes, or until beef is tender. Serve hot with sour cream, shredded cheddar cheese, corn tortilla chips, and chopped scallions.

[Serves 6]

Black Pot Osso Buco with Porcini Risotto

If you like veal, this is the "godfather" of veal recipes. It takes some time to prepare but is well worth the wait. Classic osso buco is served with the finishing touch of a gremolata, the recipe for which I have also included. The combination of fresh parsley, lemon zest, and garlic are just the tangy bite the finished dish needs to round out the flavors.

³/₄ cup (83 g) unbleached all-purpose flour

2 tablespoons (14 g) Dry Rub Spice (recipe follows)

Salt and freshly ground black pepper, to taste

6 veal shanks (6 pounds [2.75 kg] total), cut into 1" (2.5 cm) slices

³/₄ cup (175 ml) extra-virgin olive oil

1 yellow onion, coarsely chopped, plus ¹/₂ cup (65 g) finely chopped

1 cup (130 g) diced carrot

1 cup (120 g) diced celery

3 cloves garlic, finely chopped

3 bay leaves

2 sprigs fresh rosemary

2 sprigs fresh thyme

1 ¹/₂ cups (355 ml) dry red wine

11 cups (2.6 L) meat stock (beef or veal)

3 cups (585 g) Arborio rice

1 cup (235 ml) dry white wine

2 pinches of saffron threads soaked in ¹/₂ cup (120 ml) warm meat stock

¹/₂ cup (25 g) dried porcini mushrooms soaked with the saffron threads

4 tablespoons (55 g) unsalted butter

1 cup (100 g) grated Parmigiano-Reggiano cheese

FOR DRY SPICE RUB:

1 tablespoon (7 g) paprika

2 teaspoons (12 g) kosher salt

1 tablespoon (3 g) garlic powder

2 teaspoons (6 g) onion powder

2 teaspoons (6 g)
ancho chile powder

1 tablespoon (6 g)
coarsely ground black pepper

2 teaspoons (5 g) dried thyme

FOR GREMOLATA:

1/2 cup (30 g)
minced fresh flat-leaf parsley

Zest of 1 lemon, finely grated

2 cloves garlic, finely minced

Preheat oven to 375°F (190°C, or gas mark 5). Heat a large 12" (30 cm) -wide by 3 1/4" (8 cm) -deep cast-iron fryer over medium-high heat. Add the olive oil and heat until very hot. In a shallow dish combine the flour with the Dry Rub Spice and dredge the veal shanks in the flour, coasting thoroughly. Shake any excess flour off the shanks. Place the shanks in the hot oil and cook until well browned on all sides, working in batches if necessary. Remove the shanks to a dish and set aside. To the hot pot, add the onion, carrot, and celery. Cook until tender and lightly browned, 4 to 6 minutes. Add the garlic, bay leaves, rosemary, and thyme; season with salt and pepper; and cook for 1 additional minute. Add the red wine to the pot and deglaze the pan, scraping up any browned bits from the sides and bottom of the pan. Cook down until reduced by half, 3 to 4 minutes. Add 5 cups (1.1 L) meat stock and bring to a boil. Reduce heat to low, return the veal shanks to the pot, cover, and cook for 1 1/2 hours, or until the shank is very tender.

Meanwhile, prepare the risotto: in a saucepan over medium heat bring the

remaining 6 cups (1.5 L) of meat stock to a gentle simmer, and maintain over low heat. In a large heavy skillet over medium heat, warm the remaining 1/4 cup (60 ml) olive oil. Add the 1/2 cup (65 g) finely chopped onion and cook until tender, 4 to 5 minutes. Add the Arborio rice, stir, and cook until each grain is translucent with a tiny white dot evident in the center, 3 to 4 minutes. Add the white wine and stir until completely absorbed. Add the warm stock to the rice, a ladleful at time, stirring frequently after each addition. Wait until the stock is almost completely absorbed before adding the next ladleful, reserving about 1/4 cup (60 ml) of stock for the end. After about 20 minutes, the rice will be tender with a slight firmness to the bite. Add the saffron-mushroom mixture, stirring to combine. Cook until the liquid is absorbed, 2 to 3 minutes. Add the butter and cheese and season with salt and pepper, stirring to combine. Add the reserved 1/4 cup (60 ml) of stock, remove from heat, and keep warm until ready to serve.

Once the shanks are tender, remove from the oven and serve hot with the risotto and pan sauce.

[For Dry Spice Rub]
In a small bowl, combine all rub ingredients.

[For Gremolata]
Combine the three ingredients in a small bowl. Serve as a garnish over the top of each veal shank.

Cornmeal-Fried Oysters with Chipotle Cream

South Texas oysters are tender and sweet and great right out of the shell. However, some people just don't have the appreciation for raw oysters, so I offer this fried alternative. Don't be put off by what may seem to be a troublesome dish to prepare, as it is quite easy and makes a great appetizer. If you don't have the inclination to shuck your own oysters, ask your fishmonger to do it for you.

16 fresh oysters, shelled

2 eggs, beaten

3/4 cup (103 g) cornmeal

1/4 cup (110 g) all-purpose flour

1 teaspoon (6 g) kosher salt

1/2 teaspoon (1.5 g) chipotle chile powder

1/2 cup (120 ml) peanut oil

2 cups (475 ml) Chipotle Cream (recipe follows)

Lime wedges, for garnish

FOR CHIPOTLE CREAM:
Makes 2 cups (475 ml)

1 1/2 cups (345 g) sour cream

1/4 cup (55 g) mayonnaise

1 canned chipotle pepper in adobo sauce, minced

1 teaspoon (5 ml) lime juice

1 teaspoon (3 g) paprika

1/2 teaspoon (3 g) salt

1/2 teaspoon (1 g) freshly ground black pepper

Clean the oysters of any remaining shell and set aside. In a small dish beat the eggs and set aside. In another small dish, mix together the cornmeal, flour, salt, and chile powder and set aside. Heat the peanut oil in a small, shallow cast-iron skillet over medium-high heat. When the oil is hot, dip the oysters in the eggs and then in the cornmeal mixture. Shake off any excess and lay gently in the skillet. Pan-fry quickly, about 2 minutes per side, turning once.

Remove and serve atop a bed of greens, with chipotle cream for dipping and lime wedges.

[For chipotle cream]
In a small bowl mix together the sour cream, mayonnaise, chipotle pepper, lime juice, paprika, salt, and black pepper. cover and refrigerate until ready to use, at least 30 minutes.

Venison Chili

While I was growing up, venison was quite common around our house. It is uncommon today to find good recipes for venison, so I have provided this delicious chili as one way to prepare it. If you are unable to find good-quality fresh venison where you are, simply substitute beef, chicken, or pork.

1/2 cup (120 ml) vegetable oil

3 pounds (1.4 kg) venison shoulder, cut into 3/4" (18.5 mm) cubes

1 green bell pepper, diced

1 red bell pepper, diced

2 cups (320 g) red onion, diced

3 tablespoons (30 g) roasted garlic

2 tablespoons (18 g) chile powder

2 tablespoons (18 g) ancho chile powder

2 tablespoons (8 g) dried Mexican oregano

2 tablespoons (14 g) ground cumin

1 tablespoon (7 g) ground cayenne

1 teaspoon (7 g) ground cinnamon

1 tablespoon (15 g) tomato paste

2 cups (475 ml) beef stock

1 (12-ounce [355 ml]) bottle dark beer

1 (14.5-ounce [405 g]) can red kidney beans, drained

1 (14.5-ounce [405 g]) can black beans, drained

1 (16-ounce [455 g]) can peeled and diced tomatoes

2 chipotle peppers in adobo sauce, minced

1/4 cup (15 g) chopped fresh cilantro

Shredded aged cheddar cheese, for garnish

Sour cream, for garnish

Fried Corn Strips, for garnish (recipe follows)

FOR FRIED CORN STRIPS:

2 cups (475 ml) vegetable oil

6 corn tortillas (blue or yellow), sliced in thin strips

Heat 1/2 cup (120 ml) of the vegetable oil in a large cast-iron Dutch oven over medium-high heat. Add the venison and brown, in batches, transferring to a plate. Add the red and green peppers, onion, and garlic, and sauté over a low heat until tender, about 7 minutes. Add the remaining oil, the chile powder, ancho powder, oregano, cumin, cayenne, cinnamon, tomato paste, and browned venison meat, stirring to combine while toasting the spices for 3 minutes. Add the beef stock, beer, beans, tomatoes, and chipotle peppers; cover and simmer for 2 hours, or until venison is fork tender. Add the cilantro and season with salt and pepper. Serve the chili hot with grated cheese, sour cream, and fried corn strips.

[For Fried Corn Strips]
Heat the vegetable oil in a stockpot to 375°F (190°C, or gas mark 5). Add the corn strips in batches and fry to a crisp golden color, about 2 minutes. Remove, transfer to paper towels to drain, and season with salt.

Index

Acknowledgments

I would first like to thank our ancestors who brought cast-iron cookware through history and didn't allow time to erase what is truly a link to the past. It takes numerous hours on the part of many to compile a book of this nature and I thank each and every one of those involved. To Winnie Prentiss, publisher, and Rochelle Bourgault, project manager, I offer my deepest regards for their patience and willingness to endure these projects with me. To Rosalind Wanke, art director, for her guiding presence and artful touch that she brings to my books. Without her, I am not sure this project would have become the beautiful work that it is. To all of those at Creative Publishing international, I thank you for the beautiful photos. These pros brought their exacting touch to every image. Thank you, as always, to my many family members and friends who inspire, encourage, support, and praise me on a regular basis.

Thank you, too, to all of the readers and chefs who buy these books. As with all of my books, I write this as inspiration to you to find the creativity inside to bring good food to the table.

About the Author

Dwayne Ridgaway, a native of Kerrville, Texas, lives in Bristol, Rhode Island. He is the author of the well-received *Lasagna: The Art of Layered Cooking*; *Pizza: 50 Traditional and Alternative Recipes for the Oven and the Grill*; *Sandwiches, Panini, and Wraps: Recipes for the Original "Anytime, Anywhere" Meal*; *Indoor Grilling: 50 Recipes for Electric Grills, Stovetop Grills, and Smokers*; and *Perfect One-Dish Meals: 50 New Tastes for Old-Fashioned Comfort Food*; as well as contributing author, food stylist, and recipe developer for several notable magazines and books. Dwayne, a graduate of Johnson and Wales University, currently works as a food and beverage consultant, caterer, and event designer. He has, in short, made a career out of exploring and celebrating the culinary arts. His passions drive him to develop fresh recipes that any reader can execute and enjoy. Dwayne's goal is for all readers to use his recipes and writing as a groundwork for their own personal creativity.